AN OUTLAW'S JOURNAL

The events in this story are drawn directly from fact.

First Printing, 2023

ISBN (print edition): 9780645378429
ISBN (eBook): 9780645378436

Front Cover: "Butcher's Shamble. F. Creek" by S. T. Gill (c.1852) [Courtesy: State Library Victoria; H12537-12539]
Back Cover: Beechworth (c.1873) [Courtesy: State Library Victoria; 9917155733607636]

ALSO AVAILABLE FROM THIS SERIES
Ah Nam (ISBN 9780645378405)

COMING SOON
Blood and Bamboo
The Temptations of Joe Byrne
The Horror at Sebastopol

AN OUTLAW'S JOURNAL

〜∞〜

Joe Byrne and the Cow from El Dorado

GEORGINA STONES

Illustrated and Edited by Aidan Phelan

Australian Bushranging

Contents

PROLOGUE

ACKNOWLEDGMENTS

BEHIND THE JOURNAL

Dedicated to

Joseph Byrne

and

Aaron Sherritt

And the people of Beechworth, Sebastopol and El Dorado who feature
within the pages of this book.
And, of course, to my fiancée, Aidan Phelan.

A Note from the Author

To my dear reader, what you are about to consume is a dramatised narrative based on my historical research. I believe that this is a way to make the past more vivid and relatable for those of us that were not there in a way "straight" non-fiction cannot. It is also a way for me to contextualise the broader research that I have done in a way that shows how it relates to the history without being dry or distracting the readers from the core of the story. All too often in traditional history books the author will side-track the reader with footnotes, sidenotes and appendices, and we end up losing our place in the story. Now everything will seamlessly blend together for your enjoyment as much as your education.

But for those hoping for a "facts and figures" approach to history, never fear — following the narrative you will find a summary of my research, how it relates to what you will have just read, and even some of the source material transcribed for you to read. It may have taken months — years, in fact — for me to find and compile this information, but for you it is all in this one convenient location. You will see that what I have written is no mere fantasy but rather an informed interpretation of everything I have discovered to date about Joe Byrne, those who were a part of his life, the places and times he lived in, and the reality of what happens to a young man faced with the many challenges, temptations and disadvantages he faced during his brief time on this earth.

Without further ado, I invite you to enjoy your journey into the past as you delve into the following pages. I know that I have enjoyed writing them for you.

— Georgina Stones.

Prologue

Under a hot January sun, Joe Byrne and Aaron Sherritt slowly trudge along the dusty road called Camp Street in Beechworth. The strawberry-coloured calf they are leading has made the long journey from Sheepstation Creek, regularly stopping to sulk and call for its mother. The animal is unbranded, but Aaron promises it is one of his own. Joe, however, has his doubts. He knows his mate's weakness for lifting livestock and the thrill it generates; it has become almost an addiction for the 20-year-old, Aaron's own version of the peace from smoking sticky black opium tar that Joe craves.

Arriving outside James Warner's slaughter yard, Aaron mindlessly throws Joe the rope and swaggers into the yard, swatting the blowflies that hover over his chin.

"I'll go and see if I can cut Warner a deal," Aaron calls over his shoulder before disappearing under the awning.

Joe nods and pulls the brim of his porkpie hat over his eyes, wary of curious eyes that may spot him holding an unbranded calf outside Warner's yard. Aaron may be cavalier about the prospect of being caught for his duffing, but for 19-year-old Joe, prison was the only place that genuinely frightened him — the thought of being locked behind granite walls with gaol-hardened men, at the will of ruthless turnkeys, with nothing but a sledge hammer and rock to pass the hours. It was a world away from his own in Sebastopol and one he did not wish to be thrown into, least of all because of Aaron.

Suppressing the thoughts, Joe pushes them to the back of his mind, leaving them to lay with the other worries that come from following Aaron, and gazes towards the intersection of Camp and Ford Street. The echoing shouts of the auctioneer of Gray and Co. carry along the warm breeze, signalling the start of the Beechworth horse sales.

"Oi, Joe," Aaron suddenly calls, "stop daydreaming and bring the calf in."

Joe sighs at the order and tugs on the rope. The calf braces itself against the pressure and shakes its head, foamy saliva spraying from its mouth.

"Come on you bloody thing," Joe growls through gritted teeth, "I'll have it worse than you."

The calf's hooves scuff against the loose granite of the road as Joe pulls it into the yard.

"You'll have to forgive her," Aaron says, smirking at Joe as he struggles with the defiant heifer, "she's had a long journey."

Joseph Harvey, James Warner's slaughterman, points a grubby hand towards one of the yards, his calico apron stained with streaks of crimson. "That yard there will do. And keep the rope on her, if you don't mind."

Joe nods and herds the calf into the small yard, stepping over the cow pats that are alive with the buzzing of flies. Affixing the rail, Joe looks at his palms, a stinging red mark visible from the abrasive rope.

"You could have carried her in," Aaron jibes with a smirk.

Joe curls his lip into a grimace and rubs his palms on his moleskin trousers.

"You better be telling the truth about this calf Aaron," he asserts bluntly, "or you'll be finding yourself down a mineshaft by morning."

Undaunted, Aaron laughs at the threat and swaggers toward James Warmer as he emerges from a slab outbuilding, his record book tucked tightly beneath his arm.

"I've made a note of the sale price and agreement in my book, Mr. Sherritt. I will have the head and hide for you in around an hour."

"You're too kind, Mr. Warner. I know Da will appreciate the hide for whips and Ma the head for cooking."

Joe's blue eyes widen at the 'agreement', aware it is required for butchers to keep a hide in their possession for at least one month; a law that is enforced so inspectors of slaughter yards are able to maintain everything is done above board. While Joe himself is not above taking what is not his from time to time, he certainly knows better than to lead a stolen calf into Beechworth and demand the unbranded hide be given back to him.

"Ah, it's no trouble," James answers, rubbing at his sweaty brow, "I'm without pigs at the moment, so I am glad I won't have to tolerate the smell. Especially in heat like this."

"Well, it's a pleasure doing business with you again, Mr. Warner," Aaron remarks with a flourish of his beaten porkpie hat.

James shakes Aaron's hand and looks to Joe. "And your mate is...?"

"Byrne," Joe answers, distracted by thinking about how he is certain it will not be long before Aaron's foolishness lands them both in chains.

"Good to meet you, Mr. Burns," James says, offering his hand. Joe doesn't correct him.

I

Following the course of Stony Creek as it runs along the other side of Byrne Gully, Joe and Aaron walk through the bush, heading for Aaron's selection at Sheepstation Creek. The smell of eucalyptus hangs thick in the air as a kangaroo bounds through the undergrowth, spooking the two stolen fillies they lead, recently branded in Edward Kennedy's abandoned yard, which lies behind the Byrne selection.

With each step, Joe's moleskins painfully rub against a bloodied gash on his pale shin. He stops and rolls up the fabric of his trousers and long johns, the cold air stinging the wound.

"She's got some strength to her," Joe remarks, looking at the wound.

Aaron grimaces at the gleaming gash, "You can use that as your bill of sale."

Joe rolls his trouser leg back down and resumes walking, the filly skittishly following.

"You wouldn't be sounding so smart if you'd been the one that she bloody took to."

Aaron thumps his mate on the back. "Only having a lark, Byrne. Besides, I have a proposition to make."

"What would that be?" Joe asks, cautious of getting himself involved in yet another of Aaron's schemes.

"That school cow over at the El Dorado Common, the one from old Dick Maddern's herd, I reckon we would be able to take her, easy as we please."

Joe shakes his head. "You won't be satisfied until you have us both in gaol, will you?"

***

Arriving up at their secret yard, Joe and Aaron free the fillies from their halters, watching as the young horses canter around the enclosure in the fading light.

Joe lifts a shovel from where it is concealed between jagged wedges of rock and digs it into the muddy earth until water begins flowing through the trench. One of the fillies drops her head and sniffs at it, the water rippling from her breath, and begins slurping it thirstily, her ears flicking back and forward with each swallow.

"Are you coming to the hut?" Aaron enquires from the gate, the halter looped around his shoulder.

Placing the shovel back between the rocks, Joe walks up to Aaron.

"No. I think I might head down the gully and see Ma. It's been a while since I was last home."

Aaron gestures for the halter in Joe's hand. "Suit yourself."

***

It is nightfall when Joe finally arrives back in Sebastopol and while his plan is to head home, there is someone in particular he wishes to see first.

Crossing the footbridge of Reedy Creek, Joe passes the lantern-lit perimeter of the Chinese camp, his eyes fixed on a small hut in the distance.

Stopping outside the dwelling, Joe purses his lips and whistles, within moments the door opens, the figure of eighteen year-old Ellen Salisbury emerging.

"Joe? What are you doing here?" she asks, glancing warily back at the hut.

"Is your father home?"

"No," she answers, "he's in El Dorado at Collier's Beershop, but my brothers are inside and you know what tattletales they are."

Joe pulls her into the shadows, his lips caressing the softness of her hair.

"I want you to come with me up to Kennedy's old place," he whispers.

"Joe, we can't. Not now."

Joe rolls up the left hem of his trouser and undergarment, uncovering the blood encrusted gash.

"I'm injured, Elly."

Ellen's eyes grow large with concern. "I'll fetch some rags."

***

Joe sits in Ned Kennedy's old hut, his wounded leg propped on a stump, while Ellen kneels beside him, dabbing at his shin with a dampened cloth.

He leans forward, brushing his hands across the soft angles of her face. "My Elly," he murmurs, "I've missed you."

Ellen pauses cleaning the wound and looks up at him, the light of the lamp lending her hair a golden hue.

"I've missed you too, Joe. What on earth did you do to yourself?"

"I was with Aaron. We were branding two fillies in the yard out there and mine got a little lively."

Ellen rolls her eyes and resumes her care.

"Sherritt is a bad influence on you, Joe."

Joe reaches for her hand and squeezes it gently. "I don't want to waste time talking about him, Elly. Not when we have so little time together."

Ellen's expression becomes sadder.

"Martin came to the house today," she says, changing the subject of their conversation, "he was making all kinds of promises to father about the husband he will be."

Joe straightens his leg, wincing against the pain as Ellen dabs the wound with iodine.

"I don't want to talk about *him* either."

Ellen places the cloth back into the pewter dish and rises from the floor.

"We cannot ignore it, Joe. This marriage is happening next month whether we want it to or not, my feelings mean nothing to father. He was patient at first, but he's tired of your drifter ways, Joe. He wants me to settle down and begin a family of my own."

"Martin Byron is nothing more than a drunkard, with more enemies than friends," Joe scowls.

"I know that, but father thinks otherwise," replies Ellen, "perhaps if you drank more and stole less it would be you I would be marrying next month?"

Joe grabs Ellen and pulls her into his lap.

"Elly, we have to steal these moments while we can. When you are here with me you are still my donah. Your father and Byron cannot change that."

"Oh, Joe," Ellen says, her eyes watery, "I love you."

Joe wipes her tears away and guides her across to an old bunk.

"I love you too, lass," he replies, laying her down.

II

The honking of his mother's geese rings in Joe's ears, waking him. It is the start of a new day. He rubs at his eyes, crusty with sleep, and rolls onto his back. His mind drifts to the previous night with Ellen, and the taste and smell of her, which lingers on him.

Knotting his fingers behind his head, Joe stares up at the sheet of calico that passes for a ceiling as the wind whistling through the gaps in the timber cause it to billow. He contemplates the day ahead.

His absence from home has long been a sore spot between Joe and his widowed mother, Margaret. The hut on Aaron's selection, while initially built to appease the land act, had lately become Joe's home. It serves as a refuge where he can be alone, away from the disapproving gaze of his mother. Their relationship had long been fractured and Joe was unsure how, or if, it could ever be mended. On the times they had reconciled, the crack had always been visible. He saw it like a plate that has been smashed: the pieces may line up but could never be fixed. While he is aware he must mend the fencing of the cow yard, chop wood for the fire and attend to the chores the younger children are unable to do, the township of Beechworth is always calling to him like a Siren.

He wonders, *perhaps this cow Aaron has been harping on about will be the thing to repair their relationship? Perhaps it will prove to her that he still cares and wants to provide for her and his siblings?*

Joe sits up, the bed frame creaking tiredly beneath his weight, and rakes a hand through his bedraggled hair. He swings his legs out from beneath the woollen blanket and pulls aside the covering over the window beside the bed, the rush of sunlight catching the dust that floats throughout the partitioned room. He looks out the window, his gaze settling on his two younger brothers, Patsy and Denny, while they complete their morning chores. He feels a pang of guilt as he watches Patsy working on the cow yard. *A job that should be undertaken by him.*

Setting the room back in murky darkness, Joe rises from the bed and reaches for his moleskins and brown crimean shirt, while from behind the partition his young sister Mary coughs from the late autumn chill.

The young girl presses her face into the fabric to get Joe's attention, a habit she had developed since Margaret had chided her for slipping through the partition without first checking if her brothers were decently attired.

"Are you in your clothes, Joe?" Mary asks, sniffling.

Joe quickly dresses and begins tying the laces of his bluchers.

"I am, Mary."

His sister pokes her head through the join in the curtain, her nose red from the cold.

"Ma will be cross that you're still in bed," she begins, "but I'm not. I like it when you are home. You don't tease me like Denny does."

***

Joe soaks a washcloth in the water from a small copper basin and looks into the small mirror at his sleep-lined reflection. Wringing the excess water, he sponges the cloth across his face and neck. Picking up a small comb, he brushes it through the tangles in his auburn hair and runs its teeth through the wisps of his sideburns.

Slipping his waistcoat over his shirt, Joe ties his neckerchief around his throat then takes his jacket from the hook and makes his way down the newspaper-lined hall.

Joe takes a spot on the bench seat of the dining table, while Margaret stands in front of the hearth stirring a wooden spoon through a bubbling pot of porridge. Sitting across from him is five year-old Ellen, Joe's youngest sister, an expression of curiosity painted on her face.

Joe smiles at his sister and brushes a curl back from her face.

"It's me Ellen, your big brother Joe."

She nods uncertainly, her blue eyes scanning his face unknowingly as if taking in a stranger, which to her, Joe knew he was.

"I am surprised to see ye here," Margaret begins, her County Clare accent tinged with resentment, "I was sure ye'd have already ridden up to Sherritt's."

She spoons porridge into a dish and places it in front of Elly, who stretches her arm across the wooden table to where a collection of spoons lies.

Joe picks up the metal utensil and passes it across to his sister.

"No, Ma, I thought I'd spend the day here on the selection and see what I can help with. I see Patsy's been adding timber to the cow yard."

"He has," she replies, handing Joe a steaming bowl of porridge, "Patrick is always a great help to me. I don't know where I'd be without him."

"You know I would help you more if I could," Joe says quietly, guilt lacing the words.

Margaret loosens the drawstring of her apron and removes it from her waist.

"I find that difficult to believe," she sighs, folding the grey apron in half in her hands. "It is by choice that yer never around to help."

Joe rubs his forehead where he feels tension rising.

"Ma, I've told you before, Aaron has no one else to help him fence his selection except Jack, and he is tied up with his own land, leaving it all to be done by Aaron and I."

Margaret purses her lips and takes a spoon from the centre of the table, planting it in the mush of oats in front of him,

"That's not yer concern, Joseph. Yer concern should be here, with yer family."

Joe looks away from her gaze to the porridge.

"If Aaron doesn't keep up the improvements, he'll lose it."

Margaret thumps the table with her fist, the violent action causing young Ellen to whimper.

"And what about my selection, Joseph?" she snaps, spittle spraying from her mouth, "What is to happen with that? While yer digging new posts for Sherritt, mine are all rotting!"

Joe picks at a patch of dead skin that is flaking on his thumb and remains silent. *What could he say? What will happen to her selection if he does not step into his father's boots and become the man of the house? Why was he so unable to put into words the thoughts in his mind?*

Margaret shakes her head and cuddles Ellen in an attempt to soothe the young girl's tears.

"I suppose I shouldn't expect any less, ye've always had a lazy streak. Yer father is at fault for that. But at least he knew the value of blood."

***

With his mother's words fresh in his mind, Joe readies a log on the chopping block and plunges the axe blade down through it, splitting it unevenly. He is determined to prove her criticisms wrong. He repeats the process, the dull sound mixing with the animated noises that envelope the flat.

Beside him, his brother Denny works busily picking up the halved pieces of firewood, tossing them into their father's old wheelbarrow.

"It's nice to have you here, Joe," Denny remarks, kicking away loose bits of bark, "Paddy never lets me help him with the firewood."

Joe removes his corncob pipe from his mouth.

"Why is that?"

"He says I'm too careless when I fill the wheelbarrow."

Joe looks at the barrow, filled haphazardly with wood, and shrugs.

"All this has to be restacked against the house anyhow. I see no problem *how* you fill it, as long as you do it."

Denny rolls up his sleeves and grins at Joe's approval.

"I'll tell that to Paddy next time."

Joe laughs and ruffles his younger brother's hair.

22 ~ GEORGINA STONES

"Aye, you do that."

***

While Joe works with the axe, a figure on a chestnut horse suddenly catches the corner of his eye as the unknown horseman canters closer towards him. Joe looks up and removes his porkpie hat, wiping away the beads of sweat that cling to his brow.

He eyes the red sash that is bound around the rider's waist.
"Aaron?" He quizzes under his breath.

Joe takes a step back as Aaron wheels his mare around and halts in front of him, grass coloured foam dripping from her mouth as she chomps at the Tom Thumb bit.

"I haven't caught you doing honest work, have I Joe?" Aaron laughs, rubbing comically at his eyes, the leather of the saddle creaking as he stoops over the mare's neck to look at the wood in the barrow. "Oh, hang on, I bloody well have!"

Joe wedges the axe blade in the log and straightens, unable to see the humour.
"If you've only come to give me cheek, you can bloody leave. I've already had Ma on my case this morning about how I'm never here."

Aaron swings his feet out of the stirrups and dismounts, looping the leather reins over the fencepost.
"I suppose you're going to blame me for that?" he asks, pushing his mare's head away as she attempts to rub her bridle against his back.

Joe removes the pipe from his mouth, curls of smoke drifting into the crisp air.

"Well, it is your damn selection I'm helping you fence."

Aaron pushes his hat back and steps closer to Joe, his hazel 'laughing' eyes crinkling at their corners. He ignores the remark.

"Remember how I was telling you about the heifer over at the El Dorado Common? The one that's under old Dick Maddern's watch?"

"Aye, I remember," Joe sighs, shaking his head. "I told you it was a damned fool idea then, and I'm standing by it, Aaron."

"Ah, come off it, Joe," Aaron hisses, prodding him in the shoulder, "when did you turn into such an old woman?"

"I'm just trying to get you to see some sense. You were bloody lucky that Constable Mullane didn't pin you for that hide back in January. You know how close he came to lagging you. He certainly made it hot for James Warner. You read it all in the paper."

Aaron brushes Joe's concerns aside with a sweep of his hand and bends down to grasp the lump of firewood at his boots, tossing it into the wheelbarrow. It rolls off.

"That bugger won't catch me," he replies defiantly, picking a splinter from his thumb.

"Jesus, Aaron..." Joe mutters, turning away to watch Denny as he chases Mary with a strip of bark. Her excited squeals echoing across the flat as she runs behind the stable.

Margaret's voice suddenly cuts through the valley, as she calls sharply from the clothesline.

"Dennis Byrne! Stop tormenting yer damn sister!"

Aaron raises his eyebrows and stifles a laugh.

"You want your Ma to stop hounding you?"

Joe nods and sucks on his pipe.

"Well then," Aaron begins, with an air of authority, "bringing her some fresh beef should do the trick."

Joe looks across at his mother, her frame seems small while she pegs undergarments on the string line. He shakes his head.

"She'd skin me alive if she knew it was stolen. She screamed like a banshee when I took Phelan's saddle and I wasn't even aware that bloody thing was his."

Aaron takes the axe from Joe's grasp and splits a log.

"You don't tell her, you fool," he says, throwing the log into the barrow. "We can take the cow easy as we please, put her in Kennedy's old yard like we did with those fillies and butcher her no trouble."

Joe empties the burnt plug of tobacco from his pipe onto the ground and grinds it with the toe of his boot.

"You know we could be imprisoned for this, don't you?"

Aaron slaps his hand on Joe's shoulder.

"Who said anything about getting caught, you bugger?"

***

Nearing the brick school building, Joe and Aaron dismount. Tethering their young mares in the scrub, they make their way down the small bank. As they approach the paddock, the young white cow lifts her head from the pick of grass she has been grazing.

"She's in good condition," Joe whispers.

"The kiddies keep her well fed," Aaron replies, opening the wooden gate.

Joe follows Aaron into the paddock, his eyes falling on the beast's brand.

"What about the brand?" Joe asks, nodding toward the J F that is burnt into her hide.

Aaron shrugs, unconcerned.

"We'll cut it out."

"Cut it out?" Joe repeats.

"Have you gone simple all of a sudden?" Aaron asks, "We'll have a bloody knife with us when we are up at the yard."

Joe rolls his eyes and holds the gate open, waiting while Aaron leads the heifer through and up into the scrub. Holding the rope and his reins in one hand, Aaron vaults into the saddle.

"You'll have to ride closely behind her, to keep her moving," he instructs, tugging on the rope to bring the beast closer to his mare who snorts nervously at the heifer's long, fine horns.

Joe takes his reins from where they are looped over the scrub and places them over Music's neck, bunching them in his hand on the pommel of his saddle. Sliding his boot into the stirrup, Joe heaves into the saddle, lengthening the reins as the dappled grey mare begins to prance and chomp at the bit.

"Ready?" Aaron calls over his shoulder.

"Aye," Joe responds, placing pressure on Music's side with his calf to straighten her up.

Clicking his tongue, Aaron edges his mare into a walk. The heifer follows for a few steps then stops, pulling back against the rope. Reaching for a branch of wattle, Joe breaks it and rides Music up close beside the beast, as she stands, braced against the taut rope, her white tail flicking back and forth.

"Get on!" Joe hisses through gritted teeth, slapping the branch down across the animal's back, sending her jumping forward.

***

The mounting afternoon shadow stretches along the gully, as Joe and Aaron dismount behind Ned Kennedy's abandoned milking yard. Tethering their horses to the length of moss-covered paling, they lead the young white cow into the stockyard. Taking an old knife from his saddlebag, Aaron waves it at Joe.

"Lucky, I came prepared, isn't it?"
Joe stares at Aaron in disbelief, his eyes running over the blunt blade. "That bloody thing wouldn't slice a loaf of bread, you fool."
"Eh?" Aaron mutters in ignorance, rolling up his sleeves to display freckled forearms.

Joe grasps the knife from his mate, "I will not let you use this bloody thing," he growls angrily, throwing it in the mud. "This has to be done properly Aaron. It has to be a swift cut. You cannot saw at the animal's throat as if it were a log of old ironbark."

"Oi, *I'm* the one with the slaughtering licence," Aaron retorts, pointing a finger to his own chest, "don't you think *I'd* be the one to know about knives."

Joe looks into his mate's eyes with a narrowed glare. Even though he is a few inches shorter than Aaron, he is never afraid to stand his ground.

"No, you *had* a licence until Constable Ward and his long nose came sniffing around your yard and revoked it. Then you tried using Ah Loy's name and that got revoked because you're not Chinese!"

Aaron shoves Joe backwards.

"You got something better to use then, Byrne?"

"No. You'll have to go and get a better knife. After all, this entire thing was your daft bloody idea," Joe says firmly.

Aaron shakes his head. "I ain't riding up the gully to get a different sodding knife. It'll be dark soon, then where will we be?"

Joe steps closer to Aaron, his voice a low hiss.

"You use that knife on this beast Sherritt, and I'll cut you like a calf!"

Aaron shrugs undeterred, "If you want to use a different knife, go and get one."

***

Not wishing to quarrel further with his mother, Joe rides past her selection and the surrounding Chinese huts, halting Music outside the weatherboard homestead of Archibald and Jane Batchelor, and dismounts. While he finds Mrs. Batchelor to be difficult, her husband is a kindly man and had provided Joe with work after his father had died of heart disease in the late spring of 1870. However, on this occasion, it is neither of them he wishes to see behind the door, but his sweetheart Ellen Salisbury, who works for the couple as a house servant.

Joe raps his knuckles against the door.

"Please be Elly," he whispers.

Before long, one of the lace curtains of the front windows is swiftly pulled across, exposing the stern face of Jane Batchelor as she peers through the glass at him. Joe attempts to hide his disappointment with a smile.

"Good afternoon, Mrs. Batchelor," he greets, in a voice loud enough for her to hear through the glass and removes his hat.

Jane turns from the window and drops the curtain back over the glass. The smell of stew wafts up Joe's nose as the door is pulled open. The darkly dressed woman looks firmly at him, her lips pursed in a thin line.

"I'm afraid Miss Salisbury is not here at the moment, Mr. Byrne."

"That's alright ma'am." Joe can feel the prickling of his cheeks blushing.

Jane crosses her arms across her bosom. "Well, what is it I can do for you?"

Joe scrunches his hat brim in his hands nervously.

"Well, you see ma'am, I've got a calf down a hole on Limeburners Flat," he lies, "and therefore was hoping you'd be kind enough to lend me a knife and steel?"

Jane's eyes flick down to Joe's shaky hands and the crumpled brim. She raises an eyebrow.

"Wait here a minute and I will find what you require."

Joe paces along the veranda and looks up towards Byrne Gully where Aaron is waiting with the heifer, his vison blurs slightly from the anxiety that pulses through his veins.

"Here you are," Jane says curtly, breaking his trance, "I will be wanting them back as soon as you are done, mind."

Joe takes them from her and touches his hat brim.

"Aye, of course ma'am."

***

Dismounting in front of the Byrne stable, Joe leads Music into her box and unsaddles her. Taking a leaf of hay from the stack, he drops it over the rail of her stall.

He steps outside and submerges the bit in the water trough, rubbing away the remnants of grass that have collected in the join. Behind him, Denny whistles the tune of '*The Wild Colonial Boy*' while rubbing an oiled rag over his saddle.

Joe hangs his bridle on the brass hook in the stable.

"Now Denny, remember to rub the excess oil off, won't you?" He instructs, nodding towards the oversaturated leather. "Paddy and I have warned you before about being careless when you oil leather."

"I know, I know," Denny huffs.

"And don't take too long, it's almost time you brought the goats down from the gully," Joe adds, collecting the knives and steel.

Walking towards the house, Joe's gaze locks on his mother as she stands under the veranda, watching while young Elly runs around the tangle of thorns of a rose bush, a small wooden doll in her hand.

Margaret's hooded eyes glare at Joe as he nears the house.

"And just where in heavens name have ye been, Joseph?" she demands, "I brought scones out, believing ye to be doing honest work, and all I find is Dennis struggling alone with the axe!"

Her eyes move down to the knives and steel in his hands, the weight of them seemingly doubling under her glare.

"Whose are those?"

Joe gestures toward the Batchelor selection.

"Mrs. Batchelor's. Aaron and I have one of his beasts in Ned Kennedy's old milking yard."

Margaret shakes her head, the disappointment set on her face like the granite that juts from the gully.

"Oh, I see, away with Sherritt again."

"Ma, it's not like that, I promise," Joe begins, "we'll bring you half the carcass when we have it butchered."

Margaret gathers Elly up into her arms.

"Ye best be telling me the truth, Joseph. If the beast is not Sherritt's, ye'll have us all gaoled."

***

Making his way up behind the Byrne selection, Joe's ears prick at the sound of his name being called. He stops and turns, his eyes falling on Denny's plaid cap as he weaves through the trees.

"Joe, wait for me!" Denny shouts, his voice fighting against the sound of creaking limbs.

Joe looks up at the darkening sky.

"I can't wait for you, Denny. Bring down the goats and go home."

***

Arriving back at the yard, Aaron's chestnut mare stands sleepily beside the fence, resting her hind leg. Her left ear flickers as Joe and Denny approach.

Climbing through the rails, Joe's gaze falls on Aaron as he leans against the old milking shed, kicking his boots through the drain in the dirt.

He looks up as Joe nears. "Where the bloody hell have you been?"

Joe ignores the question and turns to his brother.
"Alright Denny, up you go and fetch those goats for Ma."

Denny crosses his arms, his bottom lip curling down sulkily.
"Can't I stay and watch, Joe?"
"Why of course you can, young grasshopper," Aaron interjects.
"No," Joe says firmly, jabbing the steel into Aaron's waistcoat.

Aaron wrenches the steel from Joe's hand. "Why can't the kid watch?"
Joe thrusts the knife handle as his mate. "Just go and collect the damn goats, Denny," he says irritably.

***

The heifer stands beside the wooden gate of the yard, wrapping her tongue around tufts of grass under the paling. Picking up the length of rope, Aaron leads the beast into the middle of the yard. He places a foot on the rope and runs the knife back and forward along the steel to hone it. The cow's tongue darts up into each nostril, her large black eyes looking warily at the scraping metal.

"Ready?" Aaron asks, throwing the steel into the dirt.
Joe nods nervously and grips his hands around the fine bone of the

heifer's horns; she shakes her head against the constraint of his grasp and snorts in frustration, covering Joe's jacket in foamy saliva and snot.

Aaron puts the knife to her throat.

"Keep her bloody head still, Joe," he exclaims, his brow furrowed in concentration.

"I am, you bastard," Joe retorts, his arms trembling.

Without any more hesitation, Aaron slices the knife into the flesh of the heifer's neck. She bellows sharply, bright crimson spraying from the laceration at her throat. Joe releases his grip on the beast's horns and jumps backwards as she sways and lands with a thud, a river of blood gushes from the gash, mixing with the dirt. A murder of crows who had been watching from the tree limbs, flies towards them and lands on the gate, cawing hungrily as blood leaches from the carcass.

Rolling a log alongside the heifer's back, Joe and Aaron prop the lifeless animal against it. Making a couple of small slices in the hide, Aaron cuts out the brand and slips the pieces into his pocket.

Joe collects the second knife from the ground and looks down toward the clearing. A redheaded figure catches his attention as it marches up the track. The stocky man is Andrew 'Sandy' Doig.

Feeling his heart sink, Joe straightens and clutches Aaron's shoulder. Sandy Doig is infamous for being the local gossip of the Woolshed Valley, with some jesting he can deliver the news quicker than the local paper. It was just their luck that his long nose would be the one to sniff them out.

"Fucking Sandy Doig is coming up the hill," he hisses, "he must have heard her bellow."

Aaron lifts his reddened face; beads of sweat roll down his forehead toward the mole on his cheek.

"What are you harping on about now?"

Before Joe can answer, the Scottish voice of Sandy Doig cuts through the uncertainty.

"Do ye call yerself a butcher, son?" he calls.

Aaron rubs the sweat away with the back of his bloodied hand, a smearing of gore staining his temple.

"What is it you're after, Doig?" he mutters.

Sandy steps forward and glances at the carcass.

"Are ye in the butchering trade these days, Sherritt?"

Joe looks to Aaron, watching as he skins down the beast's lower jaw and cuts out the tongue.

"Aye," Aaron growls, brandishing the pink muscle in his right hand.

Sandy's eyes widen at the implications of Aaron's actions and retreats from the yard, almost tripping over a rocky outcrop in his haste.

"Foolish old bugger," Aaron sniggers, throwing the tongue into a wooden bucket.

Joe watches as the Scotsman disappears back down into the line of pine trees.

"You got that knife sharp yet?" Aaron asks, holding out his bloodied hand.

Joe slaps his arm away.

"What the hell do you think you're doing Aaron?"

Aaron's brow knots in confusion.

"Eh?"

"This!" Joe exclaims, grasping the tongue from the bucket, mimicking Aaron's previous action.

Aaron's hazel eyes glance between Joe and the tongue in his hand.

"What about it?"

Joe drops the muscle back into the bucket and wipes his hands across his moleskins.

"While you were being so damned foolish, did it happen to cross that thick skull of yours that the bastard will probably be itching to bring Kennedy up here? Or worse, those two bloodhounds, Mullane and Ward?"

Aaron looks downcast for a moment, as if finally weighing the consequences in his mind, but the expression is quickly replaced by his usual air of self-assuredness.

"The old man wouldn't dare. Besides, old man Kennedy knows we use this yard for branding and cutting calves. He'll take no notice of that chattering beggar."

Joe mutters his disagreement under his breath and begins sharpening the second knife.

***

The wind-battered pine trees sway tall above him while Joe makes his way down the disused track that connects the old Kennedy farm to the Byrne section. The bucket holding the heifer's tongue and head is carried in his hand, the blood that crusts around her nose gleaming in the moonlight. Ahead of him, Aaron's mare negotiates the track, the two halves of hide draped over the saddle.

Between the sparse limbs, the selection of Chinese huts come into view, with the larger Byrne house positioned next to them, the water of the dam that lies between, animated by the 'bonk' of banjo frogs.

Nearing the fence line, the sound of hooves echoes as Denny's pony canters towards them, nickering at Aaron's mare.

"Stop your dawdling, and come and open the gate, Joe!" Aaron yells over his shoulder, as the mare begins to prance and toss her head excitedly at the sight of the gelding.

Aaron jerks on the reins, the bit rattling in his mare's mouth. "Bloody stand! It's nothing but a pony!"

Dropping the bucket on the dewy ground, Joe shifts the gate open and holds his arms out to keep the pony back.

Aaron leads his mare through the gap, leaning his weight heavily against her shoulder, in an attempt to stop her rushing through the opening.

The ruckus from the mare sends the flock of geese into a frenzy, and they begin hissing and honking from their pen at the figures encroaching on their territory.

Ignoring them, Joe passes around the side of the Byrne house, the discarded wheelbarrow and axe catch his attention, a blunt reminder of a promise made. Joe places the bucket holding the head and tongue into the empty barrow and gathers the logs Denny has left on the ground, stacking the wood with the rest, before pushing the wheelbarrow forward, the wheel trundling noisily across the uneven ground towards the stable.

Joe enters the darkened building. Music snorts nervously as he approaches her stall. Holding out his hand, he allows her to sniff his familiar scent.

"Got that lamp on yet?" Aaron's voice calls from the entrance, the jingle of his mare's bridle resounding as she tosses her head.

"Give me a minute," Joe answers, lifting the kerosene lamp from where it hangs against the wall. Placing it on the old chest, he removes the dusty elongated globe and twists the wick above the burner. Fumbling in the dark for the matchbox, Joe retrieves it from the shelf and takes out a match, striking it against his boot. The yellow flame crackles as he positions it above the kerosene dampened wick, painting the stable in yellow light. Replacing the globe over the flame, Joe holds the lamp aloft while Aaron leads his mare into the stall beside Music.

"I'm not looking forward to the brow beating Ma will give us for all this," Joe sighs, unable to shake the feeling of dread.

Aaron tugs at the pieces of hide and they fall, with a thud, on the hay covered ground.
"Ah," he responds, "she'll be fine. We'll tell her it's one of mine and that should be the end of it. What can she say to that?"

Joe glances across to his mother's house, watching while a silhouetted shadow moves behind the curtained window of the front room. He desires to be as indifferent to her as Aaron; to not feel the weight of her disapproval hanging around his neck like a yoke. But it was not something that came naturally. It was true that when away from home, Joe found it easier to wear a mask of indifference, but when in her presence, the mask shattered, exposing the timidity beneath.

"I'll go and cut off the horns and ears," Joe says, gesturing with the bucket lifted.

"Why?"

"They are as distinguishable as the brand. Didn't you realise that in all your wisdom?"

Aaron ignores the grumpiness in Joe's voice.

"Do what you like but be quick. We still need to bring down the four quarters of beef."

***

The door of the milking shed squeaks on its hinges, as Joe kicks it open. Locating the shallow zinc basin, Joe lowers the tongue and earless and hornless head onto its surface. He steps out of the shed and gazes up at the moon as it is slowly masked by a drifting cover of cloud, and leans against the slab wall of the shed, the cold air nipping at his neck. He blows out the light from the lamp and closes his eyes, listening to the piercing shriek of plovers as an argument erupts in Cantonese from a group of miners in the direction of the Chinese camp.

"All this damned nonsense," Joe whispers, opening his eyes as Aaron sidles up beside him with the handcart, "that cur Sandy Doig will have us lagged by sunrise."

***

The quarters of meat having been salted and hung in the larder, Joe immerses his hands in the wash basin under the veranda and scrubs at the blood that is crusted over his fingers, the murmured voices of Aaron and his sister Kate slipping under the gap between door and dirt. Joe dries his hands on a threadbare cloth that hangs from the edge of the bench, and turns the brass handle of the door, feeling the press of warmth immediately as he steps inside.

Removing his hat, Joe hangs it beside Aaron's on the hook and turns from the door, his eyes falling on the side table on which sits a Bannock cake partly covered in muslin.

"You've been busy I see, Kate," Joe gestures, disguising his angst.
Kate follows Joe's gaze and glances towards the table. "No, not me. It was made by Mrs. Feely from the Black Springs. Are you hungry?"
Joe nods. Kate cuts a wedge from the flat circular cake, spreads a layer of butter over the slice and passes it to Joe.

"Where is Ma?" he asks, biting into the dense cake.
Kate gestures towards the darkened hallway, "She's tucking little Elly into bed."

Hearing the voice of her big brother, Mary emerges from the hall, her linen nightgown sweeping over the floorboards.
"Joe!" She laughs and rushes across the small room. Joe holds his arms open, his younger sister burying herself into his chest, he pats the top of her head and sits at the table beside seven year-old Maggie, a small bowl of mashed potato is positioned in front of her, splodges of it trailing from the bowl to the edge of the table.

She smiles widely at her brother, exposing two recently lost front teeth.
"Ma made me potato snow," she gabbles through her gums.

"Well," Joe answers, leaning forward to brush a strand of copper hair from her mouth, "you be a good girl and eat that up for Ma, won't you?"

Maggie nods and digs her spoon deep into the potato, tipping half of the mash onto the table before it has a chance to reach her mouth.

"Here", Joe says, taking the spoon from her and tapping it against the rim of the bowl, "you don't need to take so much."

"Wouldn't young Joe make a first class Da," Aaron interjects with a wink.

Joe ignores the remark, his attention taken by his mother, as she enters the room.

"Where's Denny?" Joe asks.

Margaret removes the wooden spoon from the iron pot, resting it on its brim. "He's asleep, Joseph," she replies, reaching for a plate "it has been a big day for the poor soul. He's never been made to chop so much wood on his own before."

Joe takes the steaming plate from Margaret, shards of fire light reflecting in her cold, narrowed eyes.

"My intention was to chop the firewood," he explains, searching her face for understanding, but he would have more success searching for water during a drought.

Margaret raises her hand. "Ye don't need to explain anything to me, Joseph," she replies bitterly, "it is Dennis who deservers yer explanation."

***

With the stew eaten, Joe slides the knife and fork onto his plate and pushes it away from himself, the plate scraping across the wooden top of the table.

"Finished, Aaron?" Margaret asks, pointing a finger toward the plate resting precariously on his knee.

Aaron steadies it with his hand, "Aye, Mrs Byrne, but I can clear it away."

"Leave it for me you mean?" Kate jokes, rising from the table.

Aaron raises his arms in vain protest while she takes the plate, "Give a man a chance, Katie."

Scraping the bones into a dish, Margaret submerges the gravied plates into the basin and reaches across the table for Joe's, but Aaron stops her.

"I'll take this one, Mrs. Byrne," he says with a show of gallantry, "that was a grand bit of oxtail you had there."

"Yer welcome, Aaron," Margaret replies, taking the plate from him, "Paddy received the tail as payment for a cart of wood he delivered to James Chappell."

Aaron sits himself back down beside Kate and takes her hand, patting it gently.

"You will all be right for the winter with the beef Joe and me brought down for you."

Margaret hands a washed plate to Mary for drying and turns to Aaron.

"Is the beef from one of yer beasts then, Aaron?"

Aaron's eyes briefly flick to Joe, before meeting Margaret's.

"It knocked up coming home from Barambogie, Mrs. Byrne." he begins with confidence, "when I had it in Kennedy's yard, I tore Joe away from his chores, and we killed it."

"Is that the truth?" Margaret asks, sceptically.

Joe glances toward Aaron, his expression unwavering, "It is."

Margaret turns to Joe, knowing he would be the one to falter under the lie.

"The beef is Aaron's?"

Joe clears his throat, "It is Aaron's, Ma."

She gazes hard at him and turns to face Aaron.

"I don't believe either of ye."

Joe feels his heart sink. The atmosphere in the hut turning cold, despite the crackling heat of the fire. Margaret turns her back on them and mutters in Gaelic. She begins scrubbing the remainder of the plates, her knuckles growing white under the pressure of her grasp.

Finishing the final plate, Margaret wipes her hands against her apron, "Would you carry the dishwater outside, Joseph?"

Joe nods and rises from the table.

"Certainly, Ma."

Lifting the copper basin of soapy water, he moves towards the door, while Margaret wraps her woollen shawl tightly around her shoulders.

She removes the iron bolt from the door and swings it open, a press of cold air meets him as he steps out into the night.

Joe moves out from the veranda and turfs the murky water out onto the grass, while his mother's voice cuts behind him.

"Do ye realise ye could have me sent to gaol, Joseph? Do ye have any idea of the trouble this family will be in if the meat in the larder is found by the police?"

"Why won't you listen?" Joe pleads shakily, his voice raised, "the beef is from Aaron's beast."

Margaret lurches forward and slaps her hand across Joe's face, the force of her anger burning across his cheek like the tail of a whip.

"Enough, Joseph! Ye do nothing for this family! That is how I know the beef is stolen!"

Tears sting at Joe's eyes, but he does his best to repress the feelings, he does not flinch. Margaret shakes her head, exasperation etched into her tired face.

"I no longer believe a word that comes out of yer mouth, Joseph Byrne, ye made yer own bed," she asserts, "I never even know where ye are and suddenly ye turn up with beef from who-knows-where and a promise to help, for all that's worth." Margaret pauses, and glances up at the sky and scoffs, "Help? Ye don't even know the meaning of the word."

Joe holds out his arm, as if soothing a skittish filly in a storm.
"Ma..." Joe begins cautiously.

"I do not want to hear it," she snaps, cutting him off, "I want ye both out of here, d'ye understand? I want ye out!"

Joe stands motionless as she disappears back inside. He kicks at the dirt beneath his feet, sending a splattering of muddy earth to land against the door and falls onto the bench, his head clasped in his hands.

***

Leaning beside Music's stall, Joe runs his hand back and forth along her neck, her ears flicking towards Aaron as he stands at the entrance. Joe looks over at him, the lamplight casting jagged shadows against the wall.

"I need to relieve m'self," Aaron mutters, disappearing around the corner of the stable.

The thud of the front door catches Joe's attention. He steps back toward the middle of the stable and watches as Kate steps out from under the veranda, a lamp extending from her hand.

Entering the stable, Kate smiles sorrowfully and passes a woollen blanket to Joe.

"I thought you might be in need of this tonight," Kate says, shivering against the cold night air.

"Thank you, Kitty," Joe replies, his eyebrow raising at the thought of sharing a blanket with Aaron.

"I'm sorry there is only one blanket, Joe," she apologises, as if privy to his thoughts.

Joe shrugs, grateful for her kindness. "No mind. It's more than you had to do."

She touches his arm briefly, "I'm sorry about Ma. She does have reason to be worried, though."

"I'll never do right by her, Kitty," Joe sighs, the words jabbing at his throat.

Kate envelopes her arms around her brother, hugging him closely.

***

Sitting against the wall of the stable, Joe removes his bluchers and throws them against the chaff bag.

"I'm surprised you haven't ridden back up the gully," he says glancing up at Aaron as he returns from talking with Kate.

"I haven't got the energy to be resaddling my mare. Besides, your Ma will calm down by the morning," he drawls sleepily.

Joe motions toward the blanket at his feet. "We've only got the one blanket between the two of us."

Aaron looks toward the blanket and shakes his head. "I don't need no blanket," he declares, curling himself on the hay.

Joe pulls the wool over himself and stares at the bark roof, Aaron's snoring soon filling his ears.

III

⚭

Joe turns uncomfortably on the straw. The early morning sun filters through the chinks in the wall, stinging his eyes. He covers a hand over his face, and listens to the soft warble of magpies, their calls becoming drowned out by the rattling snores of Aaron.

Joe elbows him roughly in the ribs, "Shut up," he hisses, exhausted from a night of broken sleep.

Aaron opens an eye, his breath heavy with condensation. "Do that again if you're game."

"You make more noise than the bloody horses," Joe mutters, propping himself against the wall.

Aaron runs his fingers through the tangles in his dark hair.

"Kate's never complained," Aaron answers, with a wink, his face marked by the imprint of hay.

Joe rolls his eyes and fills his pipe. "You still got the matches?"

Aaron reaches over for his jacket and rummages through the pocket, tossing the small box onto Joe's thigh. Joe holds the flame over the tobacco, sucking the flame through the plug until it is fully lit.

"I'm desperate for a draw of opium," he sighs, smoke swirling from his mouth.

"Ah, you need to give up that brown stuff," Aaron proclaims, putting on his jacket, "It muddles your brain."

Joe's eyes flick up to the roof.
"Wouldn't do you any harm then."

***

Rubbing tiredly at his eyes, Joe's ears prick at the clattering sound that nears the stable. He looks across to Aaron who shrugs at the noise, a strand of hay protruding from his lips.

"Could be your ma? Perhaps she is coming over to apologise?" Aaron contemplates in jest.

Joe leans forward and looks out, his eyes falling on Kate as she walks towards them, carrying a tray topped with two steaming pannikins and slices of bread.

"I couldn't let you two go hungry on such a frosty morning," Kate smiles, handing Joe a cup of tea.

Wrapping his fingers around the cup, Joe sighs at the heat that radiates through the metal, warming the numbness of his hands. Reaching into his pocket, he takes out his father's old flask and pours a nip of whiskey into the steaming pannikin.

Kate frowns at the action as Joe sips on the tea, the whiskey adding to the burning on his gums.

Aaron moves to Kate and cups his hands around her face, causing her to gasp surprised.

"Aaron!" she exclaims, ripping his fingers from her cheeks, "your hands are nothing but ice!"

"Indeed, they are, my girl," Aaron laughs, encircling his arms around her waist, "I needed you out here last night, Katie. Your darling brother ain't real affectionate."

Joe shakes his head and turns, taking a piece of bread from the tray.

"What will you two be doing today?" Kate asks, passing Aaron a slice of bread, "I don't think Ma would appreciate having you hanging around."

"We'll be taking the rest of the meat up to Sheepstation Creek." Aaron replies, his mouth full of bread.

"Oh, Aaron," Kate groans, averting her eyes from the half-chewed mush of bread in his mouth.

"What?" Aaron replies, with an ignorant shrug.

Joe throws the emptied pannikin at Aaron's chest, "You eat worse than Denny!"

***

Riding over the small rocky rise, the Sherritt selection comes into view, with its two large post-and-rail fenced paddocks scattered with sheep and cattle. The line of bare cherry plum trees swaying in the late autumn breeze as Joe and Aaron near the front gate.

Dismounting, Joe and Aaron tether their horses to the hitching rail, positioned under an old red box gumtree.

"What about the carcass?" Joe asks, gesturing to the hessian bag tied around the cantle of his saddle.

"Hmm?" Aaron mumbles, his attention taken by the grazing sheep and cattle.

Joe follows Aaron's gaze. "It's rather late to be wishing you'd butchered one of them instead."

***

From under the hut's veranda, Aaron's mother, Anne, sweeps a broom backwards and forwards along an old rug. She looks up as they approach and rests the broom handle against the slab wall.

"Where have you been, Aaron?" she asks, her hands on her hips.

Aaron smirks at Joe and swaggers up the dirt path, causing a flock of speckled fowls to scuttle around his feet.

"I've been with me other family, haven't I?" he jokes, kissing her on the cheek.

"Get away with you," she laughs, and opens the door, beckoning both Joe and Aaron inside.

***

Leaning against the wall of the hut, Joe smokes his pipe while watching Aaron's sister Elizabeth scatter grain onto the earth, a flock of hens trailing behind her.

"Young Byrne," a voice from the left of him calls. Joe turns to see Aaron's father John walking towards him. "It's good to see ye," he smiles, clapping a hand on Joe's shoulder.

"How have you been, Mr. Sherritt?" Joe inquires, shaking John's weathered hand.

"I've not been too bad, son. Bit of hassle from the wife, but that's to be expected, isn't it?"

Joe smiles politely and shifts his gaze. Rolling up his shirt sleeves, John gestures towards the kitchen window. "Annie's been meaning to visit yer mother, but where does time get to, eh?"

"Aye," Joe nods, his eyes catching on eighteen-year-old Jack Sherritt as he swaggers towards them, a bright vermilion sash swinging from his waist.

Joe holds out his hand, "Jack."

Shaking Joe's hand, Jack turns to his father. "What's the story with that quarter of meat Aaron's brought home?"

John's expression turns to one of worry. "Meat? What meat, Jack?"

"He has it with him in the stable, he's preparing to bring some of it inside."

"Oh, he is, is he?"

***

Joe and Aaron stand beside the Sherritts dining table, which Anne has covered with sheets of newspaper from the *Ovens and Murray Advertiser*, the meat and hide resting across it.

The small clock on the fireplace is the only sound discernible, as John Sherritt inspects the quarter of beef in his son's possession. His heavy brow furrows.

"Who knocked the jimmy off?" he asks, running his dirt veined index finger over the white hide.

"I did that myself, Da," Aaron replies.

John taps his finger through the hole in the hide and onto the newspaper. "Why did ye slice it here?"

Aaron shrugs. "It was just where I decided to cut it."

John looks up at the pair. "Who helped yer divide the carcass?"

"I did that myself," Aaron replies, meeting his father's gaze.

John clears his throat. "What brand was the beast carrying, son?"

"My own brand, A and S with a half circle," Aaron lies calmly. "The beast was the white one that strayed a couple of months ago. We found her at Barambogie and she knocked up coming home."

John rubs at his cheek, his brow furrowed while he considers Aaron's story. He takes out a knife and slices down the hide in several long strips, obscuring the hole where the brand had been removed. He passes the strips to Aaron.

"Tie some of these over the bark on the veranda and do the same at yer hut."

"What for?"

John whacks Aaron across the back of the head, "Do ye think I was born yesterday, son? I know this beast weren't one of yer own, but what's done is done. I have no fear the constabulary will be looking for the hide of a stolen beast, and if they do pay a visit, it won't be so bloody obvious that ye sliced the brand out."

***

Arriving at Aaron's selection, they unsaddle their mares and turn them loose in the partially cleared paddock. Joe rests his saddle on the post and rail fence and gazes down toward the river, where a scraggly heard of goats pick at the tangle of blackberry bushes.

From the hut, the clanging of tools echoes as Aaron upturns an old potato box he had stored them in and places it under the bark overhang of his roof. Stepping on the box, he reaches around the jockey polls, tying the remaining strips around them.

Moving toward the wood pile, Joe collects an armful of the split timber and carries it toward the hut.

"Get the fire lit would you," Aaron grunts, tucking the ends of hide through the panels of bark.

The anger and uncertainty Joe has kept bottled up bubbles over and he kicks the box, sending Aaron wobbling unsteadily and gripping the roof for support.

Aaron jumps from the box, "What the hell was that for?"

Joe throws the armload of wood against the hut.

"You're fucking fortunate I haven't drowned you in that river for getting us into this mess."

Aaron shoves him backwards, sending him falling backwards into the dirt. The rage pulses through Joe's veins and he jumps to his feet, directing a well-aimed blow at his mate's jaw, the force of it cracking his knuckles.

Despite the pain inflicted, Aaron's swollen lip curls into a smirk. "You know you aren't capable of beating *me* into fits, Byrne."

Joe glares at him and shoves open the door of the hut, the sparsely furnished space is as he left it; a disorderly mess of bottles and clothing.

Stacking logs in the large stone hearth, he strikes a match and nestles it in between the kindling as Aaron enters, snatching a bottle of brandy that sits on the stump.

Joe straightens and throws his hat down on the bunk. He stares out of the small grubby window to a group of squawking sulphur-crested cockatoos as they land amongst the branches of a pine tree. "I need a smoke," he growls, reaching under the bunk for his opium pipe.

Lighting the spirit lamp, Joe takes a sticky bud of opium tar and holds it over the flame, turning it until it glows. He pushes the bud through the bowl of the pipe and positions himself on the floor, beneath his overcoat. He sucks deeply on the pipe, tipping his head back as he exhales.

"I had nothing but good intentions, Joe," Aaron sighs finally, scratching his boot along the dirt floor.

Joe looks across at him through the haze of opium smoke, his heart rate and breathing slowing. "It's too late now, anyhow," he sighs.

***

With aching limbs, Joe rises from the earth floor and moves toward the small window. Rubbing away the condensation, he gazes out at the horses, his eyes falling on the two mares as they canter along the fence line. Wary of what could be spooking them, Joe crosses to the door and pulls it ajar, shocked by the two uniformed figures on horseback riding towards the hut.

"Aaron," he hisses in his mate's ear, "Aaron you bugger, wake up!"
Aaron groans and attempts to turn over but Joe clutches his shoulder.
"Fucking Constables Mullane and Ward are here!"
Without further hesitation, Aaron's eyes shoot open.
"Here? Now?"

The rough wooden door clatters on its hinges as a fist is suddenly brought against it.
"You in there, open up at once!"
Aaron jumps to his feet and opens the door a crack, but it is soon forced open by Constable Patrick Mullane.

Joe stands motionless as the fair-haired constable enters the hut, his hooked nose scrunching at the musty smell of opium.

Looking past him, Joe eyes Constable Michael Ward, his polished boots glinting in the sunlight as he walks toward the hut.

Mullane scornfully scans the sparsely furnished room and reaches into the breast pocket of his jacket, removing two warrants. The Irishman shoves them toward the pair.

"Aaron Sherritt, Joseph Byrne, we wish to ask ye a number of questions regarding the meat we have recently uncovered at the properties of your parents."

Ward brushes past the Constable, his eyes widening as he notices Joe's opium pipe lying on the floor. He looks at Joe, his top lip curling upwards under his wax stiffened moustache.

"So," Mullane begins, "what can ye tell us about the meat? And I must caution ye to mind what ye say."

Joe avoids the glare of the constable's deep-set eyes, but Aaron straightens and clears his throat.

"It is my own. It was a beast from Barambogie that knocked up coming home and I put it in Mr. Kennedy's yard and killed it."

With a gloved hand, Ward removes his small notebook and pencil, opening to a fresh page.

"Do ye often use the yard for yer own purposes?" the Galway-born constable asks.

Aaron nods.

Ward taps the lead nib of the pencil on the paper.

"And what brand was the beast carrying?"

"My own, sir. A off the rump, with an S and half circle on the off-side."

The constable hastily scratches the brands in his notebook.

"And what can ye tell me about the marks in the beast's ear?"

Aaron looks toward Joe, his eyebrow slightly raised.

"She was earmarked with two holes punched in one ear," Aaron remarks casually, despite the question taking him off guard.

Ward's lips twitch at the young man's display of confidence.

"Do ye have any other cattle that are earmarked in this way?"

Aaron reluctantly shakes his head.

"No, I do not."

Mullane scoffs and gazes up at the cobwebbed roof. Ward shoots him a sidelong glance and continues his questioning.

"There were no ears or horns on the head when we found it at yer mother's, Mr. Byrne, what did ye do with them?"

Joe falters, realising Sandy Doig must have reported the heifer having the notches in her ear.

"I...I cut them off."

Ward makes a note of it in his book, the nib scratching against the paper.

"We found a quarter of beef at yer father's house, Mr. Sherritt. What did ye do with the remaining portion?"

"I left half of it at Mrs. Byrne's. The other quarter is there also, we were going back for it later today."

"The Constable and myself also located several pieces of hide at yer father's place, d'ye have the rest?"

"I sold one half to Joe for 8 shillings."

"Have you any portion of the half you gave to your father?" Mullane asks.

"I have it tied outside," Aaron asserts, "they were the bits my father cut off."

Mullane flicks his hand toward the door.

"Fetch them off."

Aaron steps out of the hut, with Mullane closely behind.

During the absence of his mate, Constable Ward keeps his eyes trained on Joe, half smirking at the nineteen-year-old's nervous hesitation.

Re-entering the hut with the strips of hide, Mullane passes them to Ward. He runs his gloved fingers over the short hairs.

"We will need ye both to come with us down to yer parent's selection, Sherritt."

***

Pulling up outside the Sherritt house, they are led into the kitchen, where the carcass and strips of the hide await them on the table.

Ward pieces the hide together like a gory jigsaw and twirls his moustache.

"Point out the brands," he orders, turning to Aaron.

"That's your business."

Mullane smacks his fist on the table, "No, it is *yer* business! Ye must show us where the brands are and how ye came to possess the meat. Or we must take ye both away directly."

Aaron crosses his arms. "If the hide was shaved, I might show you the brands."

The two men turn away, their voices hushed as they discuss what they have been told.

"Were ye with Sherritt on Saturday?" Ward asks, looking squarely at Joe.

Joe nods nervously, "Yes."

"What time did you go to Barambogie for the beast?"

"After dinner," Joe replies vaguely.

The constable shakes his head.

"No, that will not do. We are after the precise time."

Joe feels himself trembling under Ward's gaze.

"About two o'clock."

Mullane attempts to direct a question, but Ward cuts him off with a swift movement of his hand. "And precisely what time was it when ye went to Mrs. Batchelor's for the knife and steel?"

Joe doesn't answer, he knows Barambogie is roughly eight miles away. The trip there and back would have taken him and Aaron more than three hours, making it impossible for him to have called at Mrs. Batchelor's at four thirty in the afternoon.

"Are ye aware that Richard Maddern, herdsman of the El Dorado Common School, has recently reported the white heifer missing?" Ward continues, "It's marking matching perfectly with the hide in yer possession? Do ye have anything further to say on the matter, Mr. Byrne?"

Joe swallows the lump in his throat and shakes his head.

"Anything more from you, Sherritt?" Mullane interjects.

Aaron glares at the constable and straightens his six-foot frame. "I've nothing more to say to the likes of you."

"Then I must place you both under arrest on the charge of cattle stealing, to be heard later this afternoon in Beechworth."

Joe feels his heart sink. He has been arrested on minor charges before, but none so serious as this and with no way of proving anything beside their guilt, he does not hold out much hope for leniency.

The pair are marched outside, where Constable McHugh waits for them beside the cart, laden with the divided carcass, including the head, tongue and heart of the ill-fated beast.

Constable Mullane binds Joe's wrists with a length of rope, one end of which is attached to the cart, while Ward does the same to Aaron.

McHugh snaps the reins across the horse's back, and it moves into a walk, pulling the cart behind it. The rope tightens at Joe's wrists, pulling him forward.

***

For Joe, there is no greater shame than what he feels being led through the streets of Beechworth behind the cart. He keeps his head lowered, aware of the many eyes gawking at him from the street, focusing on the dull pain in his legs, which grows worse with each forced step.

Reaching the lockup, Joe and Aaron are pushed into the darkened cell, where an old drunk who has urinated on himself is snoring loudly from the corner.

"You bastard," Joe growls at his mate, "I wish I had never followed you to El Dorado."

Aaron remains silent, his arms crossed over his chest.

"Smells like piss in here," Aaron says.

***

Later that afternoon, they are eventually brought out of the cell and led across to the granite courthouse and appear before Magistrate Robert Pitcairn, each charged with, "Having in his possession part of a carcass of a certain heifer stolen from Richard Maddern herdsman of the El Dorado Common for the lawful possession of which he cannot satisfactory account on the 23rd instant at Sheepstation Creek."

Margaret Byrne watches the proceedings stoney-faced from the gallery, accompanied by John Sherritt. After the hearing, Joe and Aaron are remanded for a week, with bail offered at £50 — a high sum for these impoverished families, which neither can afford — leaving the pair to be imprisoned in the granite fortress that is Beechworth Gaol.

IV

Sitting at the large table in the remand yard, Joe keeps his head lowered over the copy of *Oliver Twist* he is reading, mindful of the journalist who stands outside the iron bars, gawping at him and the other remand prisoners as if they are animals at a zoo. The tweed-dressed man is flanked either side by turnkeys, a notebook and pencil grasped in his hand.

Joe watches him from the corner of his eye while the man begins to make notes. He tugs the brim of his hat low over his brow, feeling ashamed at his position, while Aaron paces along the length of the yard, like a colt desperate for a way out of the breaking yard.

It has been the longest day of Joe's life, with five more to come before he and Aaron learn their fate. The uncertainty of his situation eats at Joe's mind, with nothing and no one to soothe him.

As he sits with lowered head, he thinks of Ellen and that bastard Byron who is taking her from him, of his mother and her disappointment, and of Aaron and his thoughtless ploy that had led them both behind these granite walls. "*Yer made yer own bed,*" Margaret had told him, and he knows she is right. The choices he has made and his loyalty to Aaron has cost him dearly. He has lost Ellen, his freedom and the wedge between he and his mother is now deeper than it has ever been.

***

After a week in remand, Joe and Aaron stand in the wooden dock of the Beechworth courthouse, awaiting their fate. Joe listens intently to the evidence of the witnesses and cross examinations from his lawyer William Zincke, until Margaret is finally brought from the witness room up to the stand, the wooden boards creaking under her tread.

She recalls the events of the 19th of May, unable to hide the bitterness and disappointment she feels towards Joe. At the conclusion of her evidence, Magistrate Pitcairn looks towards Margaret with an expression of sympathy.

"Is your son good to you, Mrs. Byrne?"

Zincke shifts uneasily in his chair and shuffles the collection of papers in front of him, as if already privy to the answer. Joe glances down at the polished wood of the dock, unable to look at his mother while the question hangs, unanswered.

"Mrs. Byrne?" Pitcairn repeats.
Margaret Byrne shakes her head slightly, as if grappling with her thoughts.
"I cannot say."

Joe's heart sinks in his chest; *she cannot say.*

He wants to thump his hand against the rail, to plead his case, to make her understand that he was trying, *he is trying*. But it is all too late. The magistrate and the entire courtroom now know him to be a failed son.

The rest of the hearing passes in a haze, as Joe stares at the floorboards, until Magistrate Pitcairn utters the words Joe has for so long been dreading.

"As this is not the prisoners' first appearance before this court," he begins, looking over the pair's previous fines and convictions, "I will give each of you the heaviest punishment the law allows, namely, six months' imprisonment with hard labour in Beechworth Gaol."

Six month's imprisonment with hard labour. Joes vision blurs as he struggles to come to terms with the gravity of the sentence. He glances at Aaron, whose expression is unchanged, as if it is merely the rap of the cane across his knuckles.

The court adjourns and the guilty pair are led from the dock and bundled onto the awaiting cart.

***

The cart clatters through the open wooden gates of the prison and into the reception yard, where a head warden greets them.

Joe and Aaron climb down from the cart and are instructed to stand side by side, while the warden approaches them, a look of smugness and superiority cast over his stubbled face.

"Alright, listen up. Welcome to your new home, gentlemen – Her Majesty's Gaol, Beechworth. You are here because you are malefactors. The lowest of the low. You are here to be broken in like the wild beasts that you are. Do I make myself clear?"

"Yes, sir," Joe responds, feeling unsteady beneath the warden's stern gaze.

Aaron, however, is not rattled and merely offers the uniformed man a smirk.

"Oh, I see," the warder begins, "you think it is all a lark, do you?"
Receiving no response, the man stamps his heavy boot on the granite.
"Stand up straight and get that smirk off your face! There is no larking here, boy."

Satisfied Aaron is now aware of the seriousness of the situation, the warden steps back and resumes addressing the pair equally.

"Within the confines of these walls, you have one duty – to obey. You will be housed in separate cells. Each day after work in the yard you will return to a new cell. You will not speak or make noise. You will not interact with other prisoners. You will wear your hood whenever you are out of your cell. If you break the rules of this establishment, you will be punished. Your privileges will be taken away. If you continue to misbehave then you will go in the hole, and we will keep you in there at our discretion. If we feel you are creating a situation of danger to yourself and those around you, the warders will acquaint you with the business end of the billy club until you submit. You will be given meals in your cell. You will be permitted, after a time, to access reading material from the library. If you cannot read, we will teach you how. We will turn you into productive members of society, not the wretched, spineless leeches you are as you stand before me."

After the head warden's speech, they are directed to the wash yard. Joe shyly undresses; his clothes to be placed in storage and given back to him on the day of his discharge. He stands naked to be measured and examined. The record-maker looks over the slowly healing scar on Joe's left shin and makes a note of it, before instructing him to stand against the wall where painted measurements are displayed.

"Five feet, nine and a half inches," the man utters to himself, writing the same.

Joe sits on a wooden stool while a young man in a brown smock prepares his head for shaving. *Thank God Elly cannot see me like this*, he thinks to himself as the prison barber begins cutting his hair close to his scalp, leaving nothing but a covering of auburn stubble. Tilting Joe's head to one side, the barber begins shaving off his sideburns and moustache, the cold air almost stinging his hairless cheeks.

This indignity over, Joe is directed to the bath yard. Sliding into the murky water, he does his best to hide his repulsion as he lathers himself with the carbolic soap.

After drying himself, Joe is given a uniform of government issue clothing to dress in, comprising of a grey woollen jacket, moleskin trousers and neckerchief. He is designated prisoner number 13890. A calico silence hood is placed over his head and he is marched to a small cell.

The door bolted behind him, Joe looks around the cell, its furnishings consisting solely of two wooden buckets – one for drinking from, the other for relieving himself in – a small desk adorned with a bible, and a thin piece of coconut matting lying atop the hard stone floor. Joe feels a wrenching inside of him, his freedom truly gone.

This will be "home" for the next six months.

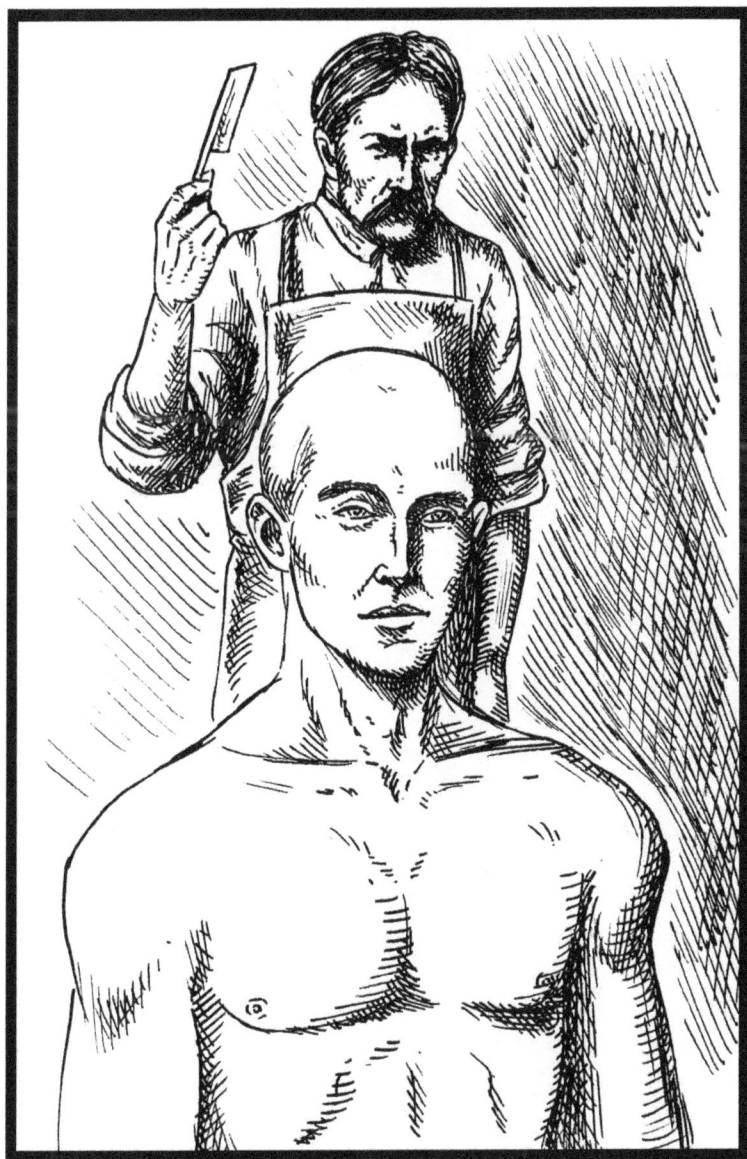

V

During the weeks he has been locked behind the granite walls, Joe's survival has been down to nothing but water, bread and gruel. Even sufficient tobacco rations have been denied him, leaving Joe to feel he must be smoking twice as much as every other cove, for he seems to be the only fellow without a plug of it to pack in his pipe.

Each day he is marched into the work yard, his face covered by the calico silence hood. From here Joe is marched to the nearby quarry to work like a dog until the break bell is rung. The cutting, crushing and hauling of rock is truly back breaking labour. He has learnt it is impossible to display fatigue since the turnkeys are ever watchful, and if a prisoner is seen to be idle they are quickly punished. Only yesterday, he was breaking rock beside a chap who had earnestly complained that the work was killing him. For his trouble, he was poked firmly in the ribs and told to keep quiet. His limbs were soon taken over by a fit of spasms and he was hurried to the hospital.

Now being winter, the days have been close to freezing and Joe has found it impossible to keep warm, but after a day in the work yard his uniform is still usually dripping with sweat. The ill-fitting hobnail boots he is forced to wear have caused his feet to become nothing but a mess of blisters and the pain he feels when walking is near debilitating. The prisoners are permitted to bathe their feet at night, but this offers Joe little relief.

He feels sure seeing men treated so cruelly amuses the turnkeys, and he knows there is one of their number for whom this is indeed true. On several occasions Joe has caught the bugger sniggering at him while he was in the act of bathing. The water was so cold and filthy when it was his turn to wash, that he found it hard to hide his repulsion. It was like the dregs of a stew pot.

The isolation has been near maddening and Joe cannot remember when he was last able to converse freely, for the turnkeys stalk the mess hall like a pack of wild dingoes waiting for the death of a tired bullock. Some of the men have tried their luck, but of course it does them no good, and on more than one occasion Joe has seen an unfortunate fellow marched to solitary confinement for having such nerve as to forget his place.

Joe's only escape is granted during his visits to the library on a Tuesday afternoon, but the selection offered is limited. Nothing like the shelves in the Public Library.

***

For Joe, it is not only his loss of freedom that weighs heavily on his mind, but the fillies he and Aaron have secured in the secret yard at the head of Byrne Gully. *He must get word out.*

While visiting the library, Joe notices Aaron, the swagger in his walk is gone, he appears slightly stooped, but the laughing quality of his hazel eyes not yet snuffed.

Joe pulls a book from the shelf and skims the pages with his finger, hoping it will be enough to awake his mate's attention. Aaron looks directly at Joe and winks as he recognises his mate's form. They stand on opposite sides of the bookshelf, not looking directly at each other.

"The fillies," Joe says quietly.
Aaron tips his head. "Write Jack," he briefly responds.

Turning his attention back towards the scant selection of books, Joe notices a prisoner hovering nearby. As he approaches the pair, Joe sees that his face is weathered, and his chin is covered in silver stubble.

"If you need something smuggled out of the gaol, I know the man," he says, sidling up to Joe, "he is a tall thin chap who works in the garden. I can give him your letter."

Without time to give what he has been told much question, Joe nods and pulls a copy of 'Wilson's *Tales of the Border and of Scotland*' from the shelf and tears the title page and fly leaf from the book, coughing to cover the sound. The unknown man passes Joe a small pencil and he begins his secret letter to Jack.

'For Johnny Sherritt Esquire,
Sheepstation Creek, Reids Creek P.O.
Near Beechworth
H.R.M. Gaol.
Beechworth

Jack I wish you would fetch a pound of tobacco to me you can send it in easy give it to the chap that is working in the garden a tall thin chap.'

Joe glances around himself, conscious of the turnkey who stands at the library's entrance.

I don't ask you to do all this for nothing. if you secure them two foals and have them and the blue filly for me when I get out I will make you a present of the best foal I have got.

Turning over the page, he continues.

You must be careful of these few pieces of paper it is very hard to get them for this is wrote on the sly and posted out of the gaol.
We must now conclude by sending kind love to all.
We remain your most affectionate brother.
Aaron Sherritt and Joseph Byrne (Well known).'

Joe's eyes glance back across the title page, the name and address he has written obscured by the text, and hurriedly rewrites it below the letter's conclusion.

For Johnny Sherritt Sheepstation Creek Reids Creek P.O
Near Beechworth

Folding the pieces in half, Joe hands them to the man, who conceals them up his woollen sleeve with a nod.

***

The day of Joe's and Aaron's discharge arrives; a day Joe knows he will never forget.

Having received the clothes he was wearing upon his arrival, Joe sheds the grey woollen prison uniform and dresses in his moleskin trousers, blue crimean shirt, neckerchief, waistcoat and jacket. After six months of rock breaking and hauling ,the fit of his shirt is not the same, with the gained muscle across his chest, back and upper arms making the fabric tighter than he remembers.

With prisoners expected to make their own way home, Joe and Aaron walk out onto Ford Street. Their hair cropped short and faces clean shaven, wearing clothes that are ill-fitting and a prison record tarnishing their characters. As they walk past the collection of granite buildings that make up the Government Camp, Joe notes the smirk has vanished from Aaron's face, replaced with a look of shame.

Joe's own thoughts turn to Ellen Salisbury. She is married now and probably pregnant with her first child. *Byron's child*. His heart aches; she is now Ellen Byron.

His mind flashes back through the events that had led him here and Aaron's promises that everything would be alright. The feelings of self-pity suddenly replaced by resentment. Resentment for a mate who had caused him so much pain.

Aaron would never put him away again.

Acknowledgments

The writing and researching of this narrative and the historical essays included within the following pages, have been a labour of love for me and one I have greatly enjoyed. The idea for the narrative first came about after my reading of the incident in Ian Jones' *The Fatal Friendship* and began life as a hastily scrawled piece within the back of a *Paperblanks* journal. Since this time, *Joe Byrne and The Cow from El Dorado* has evolved into the book you hold in your hands, and I am so very proud of that.

In terms of acknowledgements, there are a number of people I would like to thank for the inspiration, encouragement, support and determination they have brought me.

Firstly, to Joe and Aaron, for without these two young larrikins, this book would not be. I would also like to acknowledge the impact their stories have had on my life and the strength I have garnered from this. This is especially true for Joe. Not only does his life inspire me as a writer, but in telling his story I have also found a strong sense of purpose and of self.

Secondly, I would like to acknowledge Noeleen Lloyd, a treasured friend, who offers me an abundance of encouragement and guidance.

Thirdly, to my fiancée Aidan Phelan. Not only does he keep the whiskey in my glass, but he is also the biggest supporter of my work and encourages me when I need it the most. In fact, if it were not for his iced coffee analogies, this book may still have been a file on my computer. Aidan also does the fabulous illustrations that accompany my words and I am so grateful to be able to include them.

And finally, to my detractors, thank you for keeping the fire in my belly stoked and to those who threaten me anonymously, thank you for exposing what true cowardice is.

– Georgina Stones, 2022.

An Outlaw's Journal

Behind the Journal

Since reading about the June 1876 theft and butchering of the El Dorado School cow, I have been captivated by the incident and subsequent trial and have often asked myself many questions related to the events that occurred in Joe's life during that year:

What compelled him to return home after being away so long? Why did he follow Aaron Sherritt so readily? What happened between him and Ellen Salisbury? Why couldn't his mother say if Joe was kind to her? Did his time in prison change him?

Because of these questions, I wanted to write about the event in narrative form, to humanise it and bring it to life in a way that had not previously been done before. I wished to show readers what *may* have happened and the thoughts, feelings and emotions Joe *may* have experienced. I also believed it imperative to portray Joe's internal conflict and the way in which he was trapped between fulfilling the responsibilities of a son and those of a mate, and how matching up to these two ideals *may* have affected him.

Within the narrative I also wanted to portray incidents that happened within the year of 1876, such as Joe and Aaron taking the unbranded calf into Beechworth to be slaughtered by James Warner, Ellen Salisbury's marriage to Martin Byron, the fillies that were secreted in Aaron's yard and Joe's prolonged absence from home. For me, each of these events are just as important as the taking of the cow, as they provide context as to what else was occurring in Joe's life during that year and how these *may* have influenced the crime that got him and Aaron imprisoned.

I also hope, that in the reading of the narrative, it may aid in further understanding Joe and Aaron and the dynamic of their relationship. Perhaps, too, on a visit to the El Dorado Museum, which was the old school building, they will be transported back to that Saturday in June, when these two young men decided to steal the school cow.

The Trial

It is important to note how different the evidence between Margaret Byrne and John Sherritt is. One is a parent full of bitterness and disappointment, while the other is a parent willing to perjure himself for his son. Margaret's evidence is a clear window into the fractured relationship between her and Joe, and her inability to say whether he was good to her was damaging for their case. Of course, she had reason to feel this way as in her mind Joe had deserted her and even if that was not what Joe himself intended, his actions certainly portrayed this.

The evidence brought out during the trial also highlights Joe's nervousness, an aspect of his character that would continue to be commented upon during his outlawry. Coupled with this was his inability to lie convincingly, whereas Aaron was able to lie coolly and confidently, and ultimately Joe's faltering was one of the things that brought their case undone.

The following is the transcript of the trial, as reported in the *Ovens and Murray Advertiser*:

CATTLE STEALING. Aaron Sherritt and Joseph Byrne were then called on three charges amounting to cattle stealing, but the cases were withdrawn by the police. Sergeant Baber, who conducted the prosecution, then charged the two prisoners with "Having had in their possession the carcase of a certain cow on the 20th inst., at Sebastopol, for the lawful possession of which they could not give a satisfactory account and next, for "Unlawfully cutting out the brand from the hide of a certain cow on the 20th inst." Mr F. Brown appeared for the prisoner Sherritt, and Mr Zincke for Byrne, and by consent both charges were taken together as to evidence. Andrew Doig deposed that he was a miner resid-ing at the Woolshed. On Saturday, 20th May, on returning from his work at Sebastopol, about half-an-hour before dark, he passed Kennedy's yard. Before he got there, heard a beast in the yard. Saw a boy 100 or 150 yards away driving a bullock and some goats. On getting to the yard saw a cow bled and dead. The two defendants were present. Sherritt, when witness were coming up, cut two pieces of hide out of the ribs. The cow had been bled in the throat. The hide was not then stripped or partly stripped off the beast. Could not say what was done with the pieces. They turned the cow over on her back, and witness could not then see where the pieces were taken from. This was from the milking or off side. Asked Sherritt, who had the knife, if he called himself a butcher. Did not hear his reply. Sherritt skinned down the cow's lower jaw and cut out her tongue while witness was there. The other defendant then got a knife, and commenced to sharpen it on a steel. The cow looked a dirty white in colour. The horns were very fine, and a little turned in. The tip was off the right ear, and thought there were one or two cuts in the other ear, but that was in the dirt. Knew Byrne since he was a boy. He lived about a couple of hundred yards or so from the yard, but never measured it. Could not say where Sherritt resided. Knew where his father lived some miles away. There was a horse the other side of the yard with a saddle on. There was no gallows in the yard. Just stopped long enough to take a good look at the beast. Saw a rope lying in the yard. Saw no fire.

To the Bench: My opinion when I saw them cutting the pieces out of the side was that the beast was not their own. Of course, it is not usual to cut the brands out of a hide.

By Mr Brown: I saw Sherritt cut the pieces out. I could not say what he did with them; he might have put them in his pocket. The yard is not close to the inhabited part of Sebastopol; it is up between the paddock and the ranges.

There is no beaten track near it. Going towards Feely's you would come right on the yard.

By Mr Zincke: There was no prop-stick put in. There was just a log put under the beast's side. Could not say a cut was put in the beast's side to prop it up. I told Mr Ward.

Mr Zincke: Who did you tell besides?

Witness: Your Worship, am I to answer all this man's impertinent questions.
His Worship: The questions are not impertinent, but you are not obliged to answer that particular question unless you wish.

Cross-examination continued: I fancy the beast was bled when I heard the noise, and when I was about 800 yards away. I was about 20 or 30 yards off when I saw them cut two pieces out about the size of your hand.

By Mr Brown: Could not say the beast was turned over to hide where the pieces were taken out.

Jane Batchelor, a married woman residing at Sebastopol, knew the defendant Byrne, who came to her house on the evening of the 20th inst., between four and 5 o'clock. He asked her for two knives, that he had a calf down a hole at Limeburners' Flat — that is between Sebastopol and the Woolshed, some distance from Kennedy's yard. Gave him the knives and steel produced. They had not been returned to her since.

Margaret Byrne, a widow residing at Sebastopol, deposed that the defendant Byrne was her son, but had not resided with her for some time. Could not say how he was employed, excepting that he was now helping to fence Sherritt's paddock. Her son slept at her place on Friday night, the 19th. He and Sherritt went to her place on Saturday a little after dark. It might be the first time she saw them that day. They had a horse with them, but she did not see a horse. They brought home the head of a beast and the heart. They afterwards brought the whole of the rest of a carcase, and half was left with witness, a hind quarter and a fore quarter. The defendants were in company on these occasions. They also brought two knives and a steel. Could not say they were those produced, but they did not belong to witness. Saw no portion of the hide of the beast: The police did not take a piece of hide from her place. Saw the pieces of hide at the yard. Saw the carcase of the beast there. The hide was on the fence. Could not say whether it was in two or more pieces. They both slept at witness' place on Saturday night, and left on Sunday morning together about 10 o'clock. They had two horses then. They took the second half of the beast with them. They did not say where they were going. Did not think she saw them again till she saw them on Monday night at Beechworth. Her son told her the beast belonged to Aaron Sherritt. The police Constable Twomey went to her house on Sunday night, and stopped there all night. Constables Ward and Mullane came and removed the half carcase left by defendants the next day.

By Mr Zincke: I was at the yard on Saturday night; they had the beast killed then. My little boy told me it was killed. My son, the defendant, told me it was Sherritt's beast, in Sherritt's presence, and he did not deny it. The defendants told me they would leave me half the carcase when they brought it. There was no disguise about the matter that I could see; the carcase was hung up on a stick between the fence and a tree.

By Mr Brown: I know Sherritt's parents very well, and knew that Sherritt had cattle and a paddock.

To the Bench: My son, the defendant, was 19 years of age; could not say whether he was kind to me. He did not come to my place regularly lately. I have 14 or 15 head of cattle.

To Sergeant Baber: The horns were not off the head when it was brought; could not say whether the ears were on or off; could not say what became of the horns. My son took the head out next morning.

Edward Kennedy, a labourer residing at the Woolshed, deposed that he once lived at Sebastopol, and had a two-acre paddock of purchased land right on the old track, not used now. The place is abandoned. There is an old yard of his there still. Knew the prisoners. They never asked permission to use the yard. Sherritt lived a couple of miles from the yard, by a very rough road.

By Mr Brown: The yard was made for a milking yard, not for slaughtering.

By Mr Zincke: Could not say whether the defendants were in the habit of using the yard. Believe they branded a couple of calves there. Mounted-Constable Ward deposed that on the 22nd May he went to Sebastopol with Constable Twomey to Mrs Byrne's place. Found there a fore and hind quarter of beef. The head and tongue he found in a zinc vessel in an outhouse. The defendant Byrne was not present. Took possession of the meat, and about 400 yards from the house found half a hide, and the leg of a beast, from the knee down, at Kennedy's yard. The following morning, in company with Constable Mullane, went to Sherritt's father's place on Sheep Station Creek, and found some meat in the kitchen. They then went to another hut on the creek, but previous to that saw Mullane go to an outhouse with the father, and they

*immediately returned, bringing with them a portion of a hide. When they got
to the other hut asked defendant Sherritt to account for the meat they had
got at his father's place. He said, "It is my own and that it was a beast from
Barambogie that had knocked up coming home, and he had put it in Kennedy's
yard and killed it. Asked him if it had any brand. He said, yes, A off rump, S
and half circle off side, and ear marked with two holes punched in one of the
ears, and that was the only one he had with that ear mark. Asked what he
had done with the remaining portion of the meat. He said he had left half of it
at Mrs Byrne's, that one quarter was to come over yet, and that half the hide
he had sold to Joseph Byrne for 8s. Byrne was present at the time. Constable
Mullane asked him if he had used any portion of the half of the hide. He said
yes, a few strips for tying on bark, that his father had cut the strips off in his
presence. Mullane then took some strips of hide from the bark on the right side
of the hut, Sherritt saying they were the bits his father had cut off. Mullane,
witness and prisoners then went back to the father's place; and the portion of
the hide found there being produced, prisoners said it was from the beast they
killed at Sebastopol. Mullane said "point out the brands." Sherritt said, that
is your business. Mullane said, "no, it is your business to show me where the
brands are, and to satisfy me how you came possessed of the meat, or I must
take you with me." Sherritt said if the hide was shaved, he might show the
brands. Sherritt said in Byrne's presence that the meat found was part of the
beast they had killed. Asked him where the rest of the meat was. Asked Byrne if
he was with Sherritt on Saturday. He said "yes." Asked him what time he went
to Barambogie for the beast. (By Mr Zincke: Cautioned them both in the first
place.) Witness continued: Prisoner, in answer to the previous question, said he
left for Barambogie after dinner about two o'clock. Asked him when he went
to Mrs Batchelor's for the knife and steel. The distance to Barambogie would
be eight or ten miles. The nearest part would be over eight miles. Arrested prisoners, and took the hides, legs, &c., produced, into Beechworth. Asked Byrne
what he did with the horns and ears. He said, "I cut them off." The off side
of the hide had a portion missing between the back bone and the centre ribs.
The two parts of the hide fit exactly with this exception. Put the seven strips
together in presence of prisoners and Constables Mullane and McHugh, and
could not find the trace of a brand. The strip would not fill up the deficiency in
the hide. Got the knives and steel produced at Mrs Byrne's.*

*By Mr Brown: Could not say how the deficiency was, but it was in width
and length. Tried to fit the pieces in, but they would not supply the deficiency.*

His Worship said that before Constable Ward left the box, he must compliment him on the energy and sagacity he had displayed throughout the case.

Mounted Constable Mullane corroborated the evidence of the last witness, and was also commended by his Worship in a very marked manner.

Mr Brown then called John Sherritt, father of the prisoner Sherritt, and his Worship informed him by way of warning that he need answer no question which might criminate himself. The witness said his son, the defendant, would be 21 years of age in August next. For the last six or seven years he had cattle of his own, and witness knew of his son having a white cow which had strayed away some year or two ago, when it was about fifteen months' old. He heard of the beast running towards the Woolshed, and went to look for it himself. He afterwards heard of the cow being at Barrambogie, and when his boy brought the meat to his place, he represented it to be a portion of the carcase of that beast, and he received it on that representation. He himself cut the strips off the hide.

To His Worship: Was not in his son's employment. Did not receive any payment for looking after his son's cows. Went to look for his cow three times. It was all the same for him to look after the cow if the son was doing some-thing else, for they were not separated. The son and he both ran their cattle on Mackay's run, and paid for them. He (witness) paid for his son's cattle as well as his own. He was not in partnership with his son. His Worship strongly advised the witness to avoid in future tampering with the hides of slaughtered cattle. He did not think there was sufficient evidence to sustain the destruction of brands, as no brands had been proved to have been in existence, but he would certainly convict both prisoners on the other charge, and as this was not their first appearance before the court (several fines and convictions against them were read), he would give each of them the heaviest punishment the law allowed, namely, six months' imprisonment with hard labour in Beechworth Gaol. The court then adjourned.

Ovens and Murray Advertiser, 1 June, 1876. P.4

Joe and Margaret

The relationship between Joe and his mother Margaret had long been strained during his twenty-three years of life and there were many reasons for this, and one could theorise Margaret's inability to empathise with her children may have come from her traumatic background as an Irish famine orphan.

Before he drifted away from home, Joe worked a variety of jobs to help bring money to the family after his father's death in November 1870, which included working in the Chinese camp for different merchants, picking up in the shearing shed at Thologolong Station and working as cart boy for Ovens Tannery in Beechworth. As well as these jobs, Joe may have also hawked firewood around the Woolshed Valley in his father's old blue cart as his brother Paddy would come to do in 1876, trapped and sold rabbits, fenced and aided his mother in the running of her selection and 'fifteen head cow' dairy farm.

However, these good intentions would all be thrown to the wayside when Aaron required help on his selection and the siren call of Beechworth beckoned him to swagger down its cobblestoned streets. Understandably, Margaret would come to resent Joe for this, unable to say if her son was good to her in 1876, and three years later, unable to tell Enoch Downes if she would save him from the noose:

"I spoke about her own son, that she was quite right in saving him if she could; well, she hesitated about that, and she did not know whether she would or not; and there was something I was satisfied about that caused her to make up her mind that she would let her son go. She said he had made his bed, and must lie in it."

Royal Commission, Q. 13490, P.487

This was not the first time Margaret had uttered such sentiment, having expressed similar to Superintendent Sadlier in November 1878, after Joe's identity as one of the 'Mansfield murderers' had become known:

> *"We pointed out to her that her son had got his neck into a halter, and that she could save him if she liked; and her answer was — "He had made his own bed, let him lie on it.""*
> **Royal Commission, Q. 1843, P.110**

Even Margaret's use of words at the trial in 1876 highlight her feelings towards Joe, with her using the word 'son' to describe him, but 'boy' to describe Denny, while John Sherritt also used the more affectionate term of 'boy' when speaking of Aaron. In later years, Margaret would come to describe Joe as 'The Demon', when reflecting on the son she had lost. This was told to researcher Ian Jones by Joe's youngest sister Elly Byrne, who had hardly known Joe during his lifetime and so relied on other family members to paint a picture of her oldest brother:

> *"That [Joe] was the The Demon, the one we used to call "The Demon.""*
> **Ian Jones, The Fatal Friendship, 2003, P.18**

The Hut at Sheepstation Creek

While Joe was away from Sebastopol, he spent time living in the slab hut he had helped build on Aaron's selection at Sheepstation Creek. This hut would come to serve as Joe's own abode, a place where he could escape the disapproving eyes of his mother and the burden of responsibility:

"He did not come to my place regularly lately."
Ovens and Murray Advertiser, 1 June, 1876. P.4

Paddy Byrne, Joe's brother, would come to refer to the hut as Joe's while describing where Aaron was occasionally staying, during the 1879 trial for horse stealing between his mother and Aaron:

"He [Aaron] was staying at my brother Joseph's."
The Herald (Melbourne), 26 July, 1879. P.3

This hut was also where Constable Mullane arrested Joe on the 6th of February 1877 after the wounding incident of Ah On, while Aaron was arrested bark stripping at El Dorado, highlighting that Joe was still living in the hut at this time.

Joe and Aaron

An integral aspect of Joe's character was his want to follow, rather than lead and this was very much the dynamic between him and Aaron, and was something I wished to weave into the narrative. This trait is seen right throughout Joe's life and one that did come to negatively affect him. Following Aaron to El Dorado, led to him receiving six months hard labour in Beechworth Gaol, and a further week in remand in 1877 after Aaron had injured a Chinese man named Ah On, and later, when he followed Ned Kelly, it resulted in his entire existence becoming outlawed and eventually his death at age twenty-three. Furthermore, he only narrowly missed trouble when accompanying Aaron into Beechworth with the unbranded calf he had butchered in January 1876.

In conjunction with this want to follow, Joe was also extremely loyal, and his dedication to Aaron was constantly unwavering, despite the trouble it landed him. He spent months away at Sheepstation Creek on Aaron's newly acquired 106-acre selection, working hard, and unpaid, to help his mate clear and fence his property.

Even during his outlawry, when many of the gang's sympathisers had begun questioning Aaron's loyalty and motives, Joe had stuck by his mate and continued defending him, as seen in the letter he sent Aaron in June 1879:

> "The Lloyds and Quinns wants you shot but I say no you are on our side."
> Public Records Office Victoria, VPRS 4969/P0000, 18

However, the weight of continuously trying to prove Aaron's loyalty in the face of so much hate and suspicion was enough to sever the remaining trust that Joe clung to and on the 26th of June 1880 he shot and killed Aaron at his hut at the Devil's Elbow near Beechworth.

While standing over the bloodied, dead body of his once best friend, the six months and two weeks Joe had endured in Beechworth gaol and the careless attitude Aaron had exhibited to the trouble he had bought both himself and Joe flashed to the fore of Joe's mind:

"The bastard will never put me away again."

Royal Commission, Q.3657, P.180

(Author's Note: Further information regarding Aaron Sherritt can be found within my previous book Ah Nam.)

Ellen Byron (née Salisbury)

Joe and Ellen were noted to have been teenage sweethearts while Ellen lived in Sebastopol with her father James. During this time, she 'was employed as a domestic servant at Mrs. Batchelor's Hotel at Sebastopol' (*Ovens and Murray Advertiser, 29 July, 1879*) and was 'intimate with miss Catherine Byrne'. (*The Herald* (Melbourne) *26 July, 1879*)

In July 1876, while Joe was in gaol, she married herdsman Martin Byron of Chiltern and the pair went on to raise a family:

> *'Marriage. Byron— Salisbury. — At Chiltern, on the 13th July, 1876. Mr Martin Byron, son of Anthony Byron, of County Mayo, Ireland, gamekeeper, to Miss Ellen Salisbury, of Sebastopol.'*
>
> *Ovens and Murray Advertiser, 20 July, 1876. P.2*

Despite her marriage to Martin, Ellen remained loyal to Joe throughout his outlawry, risking a gaol sentence of fifteen years to support the young man she had loved. She supplied him with provisions, intelligence and shelter, and when Joe turned up on a day in May 1880 'miserable and ragged' and greatly 'in want of food', she prepared him a hot meal and beckoned him to sit by the fire. (*Royal Commission, q.13858, p.503*) This loyalty highlights that the pair were not scorned lovers, and was something I wanted to explore within the narrative. Furthermore, I wanted to show how Ellen's marriage to Martin may have affected Joe emotionally and given the context of 1876, if it had been something Ellen had wished.

*(Author's Note: Further information regarding the relationship between Joe and Ellen and her support of Joe throughout his outlawry can be found within my previous book **Ah Nam**.)*

Aaron and Ah Loy

In September 1872, Aaron Sherritt was granted a slaughtering licence, however, sometime between September and October he had lost the licence and attempted to apply for another using the name of a Chinese man he knew called Ah Loy.

'Report from Constable Ward, inspector of slaughter yards, to the Superintendent of Police with reference to Ah Loy's application for a slaughtering licence at Sheepstation Creek. The report was to the effect that Ah Loy was simply a dummy for Sherritt who had improperly used his name; the application of Ah Loy was attached to this report. The council unanimously decided not to grant the application.'

Ovens and Murray Advertiser, 2 November, 1872. P.1

Joe's Letter to Jack

While serving his 6 month sentence within the granite walls of the Beechworth Gaol, the only reprieve for Joe would have been the times when Joe was allowed a visit to the library.

On one particular visit, Joe had wished for more than just a book to read, but a letter to be smuggled to Jack regarding some stolen foals he and Aaron had secreted. It is probable that on this particular visit, a prisoner had discreetly sidled up to Joe and told him that if he wanted something sent out of the gaol, then he was the man. This particular prisoner may have mentioned there being 'a tall thin chap' working in the garden who would ensure it was sent out. It is likely that this was a trusted prisoner who curried favour with the guards and police, as the letter was handed straight to Constable Mullane, who then retrieved the foals.

Whoever this prisoner was, Joe believed what he had been told and tore a couple of pages from *Wilson's Tales of the Border and of Scotland*, and hastily scrawled a letter to Jack.

Unfortunately all that remains of the letter is a fragmented version of its original state, with a portion missing due to age and poor preservation. Luckily, enough remains of Joe's secret letter to Aaron's brother Jack that we can transcribe at least a significant portion of it. Below is a transcript of the letter as it currently exists:

For Johnny Sherritt Esquire, Sheepstation Creek, Reid's Creek P.O. Near Beechworth.

Jack I wish you would fetch a pound of tobacco to me you can send it in easy give it to the chap that is working in the garden a tall thin chap

[...] I don't ask you to do all this for nothing. if you secure them two foals and have them and the blue filly for me when I get out I will make you a present of the best foal I have got [...]

You must be careful of these few pieces of paper it is very hard to get them for this is wrote on the sly and posted out of the gaol. We must now conclude by sending kind love to all. We remain your most affectionate brother. Aaron Sherritt and Joseph Byrne (Well known).'

For Johnny Sherritt Sheepstation Creek Reids Creek P.O Near Beechworth

WILSON'S
TALES OF THE BORDERS
AND OF SCOTLAND:

Historical, Traditionary, and Imaginative.

WITH A GLOSSARY.

Revised by
ALEXANDER LEIGHTON,
ONE OF THE ORIGINAL EDITORS AND CONTRIBUTORS.

VOL. XII.

EDINBURGH:
WILLIAM P. NIMMO.

Second part

Jack I wish you would
fetch a pound of tobacco
or so to me, you can send
it in easy. give it to the
chap that is working in the
garden, a tall thin ch[ap]
come up of a fine
when he is
it in oter
right hand
as you goin
come about t[he]
next week,
Tobacco us a
all right
call in s[oon]

I don't ask you to do all
this journey — if you
secure them two fuals
and bring them and the
three fellers to me who
got out I will make you
presents of the best
I have got and

... J. Brown
and your self
... more time
... the ... other
... winter...
... God sake
... the falls

you must be careful
of those few pieces of
paper it is very hard to
get them for there is wrote
on the sly and posted out
of the Gaol. We must now
conclude by sending kind
love to all We remain your
affectionate Ford the
ran ??? Sherritt and
Joseph Byrne will ????

For Johnny
Sherritt the station
Creek Reids creek P.O
Near Beechworth

The Remand Prisoners

Although it has been stated by Researcher Ian Jones that Joe and Aaron could afford the £50 offered for bail, according to the notice within the *Ovens and Murray Advertiser* they could not:

'BEECHWORTH POLICE COURT. — *On Tuesday, before Mr R. Pitcairn, P.M., two young men, named Aaron Sherritt and Joseph Byrne, were brought up on a charge of having portions of the carcass of a bullock in their possession for which they were unable satisfactorily to account. Inspector A. B. Smith conducted the prosecution, and the prisoners were undefended. Constable Ward, of El Dorado, deposed to finding a hind quarter, a fore quarter, and part of the hide of a bullock in prisoners' possession near Sebastopol, and asked for a remand for seven days, which was granted, bail being allowed in one surety of £50 for each, but, as this was not forthcoming, the accused were locked up.'*

Ovens and Murray Advertiser, 25 May, 1876. P.2

The pair were remanded for seven days behind the granite walls of the Beechworth gaol, and while their time in remand was not recorded, we do have a snippet of what it may have been like thanks to a journalist from the *Ovens and Murray Advertiser* who was allowed entry to the gaol in 1873:

'*The next yard we visited, we found six or seven men in their usual outside-the-gaol-attire, sitting around a large table reading, these we need hardly say were prisoners awaiting trial, the rather shy looking faces, slouched heads with billy-cock hats overhanging the eyebrows, give the visitor an idea that they are as yet not altogether 'convicts' and they seemed to think so and felt ashamed of their position.'*

Ovens and Marray Advertiser, 11 July 1873. P.2

The Strawberry Coloured Calf

Beechworth Police Court. — On Tuesday, before Mr Pitcairn, P.M., James Warner, butcher, of Camp-street, Beechworth, was summoned for failing to give, on demand of the inspector of slaughter yards, a full and satisfactory account of the disposal of a certain hide on the 27th last month. Superintendent Barclay conducted the prosecution and Mr F. Brown appeared for the defendant.

Mounted-constable Patrick Mullane, inspector of slaughter yards, sworn, said that defendant kept a slaughterhouse in the Shire of Beechworth; he called on defendant at his shop in the town of Beechworth and made a demand on him on that day for the hide of a certain heifer calf slaughtered at his yard on the 21st January, but he gave no fair account of the disposal thereof; defendant told witness that the heifer calf had been brought to his yard by Aaron Sherritt and Burns to be slaughtered; that Sherritt asked for the hide, and it was given to him, an allowance being made for same in the price of the calf.

Joseph Hervey, slaughtermen to Mr. Warner, stated that on the 21st January Sherritt and Burns brought a strawberry heifer poley calf to the yard to be slaughtered, but could not say whether it was branded; they waited until it was slaughtered, and they took the hide and head away with the consent of defendant; Sherritt said he wanted the hide for making whips, and an allowance was made in the price.

Mr. Brown produced his client's books, and showed a running account with the Sherritts, in which particulars were entered of this as well as several other transactions, and that he considered a fair and satisfactory account had been given of the disposal of the heifer by the defendant.

James Warner, the defendant, in his statement, said that not having many pigs, and Sherritt having asked him for the head, he was very glad, on account of the hot weather, to get rid of it. In reference to the hide Sherritt having asked it from him to make whips, he had given it to him.

His Worship considered the account anything but satisfactory, as anyone disposing of hides in that way might steal cattle with impunity. The Act was explicit on the subject, and everyone slaughtering a beast must keep the skin for one month or give such account of it that it could be traced. He must mark his sense of this breach of the law by a substantial fine.

Fined £5. Mr. Brown asked the Bench to make it five guineas so that his client might appeal, but on his Worship signifying his assent, Mr. Warner said he would not appeal under the circumstances.

Ovens and Murray Advertiser, 3 February 1876, p.2.

A Visit to the Beechworth Gaol

(Author's Note: Parts of the following article are illegible in its original form, which I had referred to for my research, and is indicated herein by brackets. Also, included in this for context is language that is brazenly racist, so please read with caution.)

'*Perhaps there is no place where a morbidly inclined moraliser can wend his way on a Sunday afternoon, in which he may so effectually dwell upon the past and present of men's lives, and see for himself so vividly painted on the canvas of retribution, the truth of the oft-quoted maxim, "Sin and crime bring their own punishment," as he can within the walls of a criminal reformatory or a gaol; for there the branded uniforms, the manacled limbs, the worn countenances, the subservient obedience, the unearthly quiet, the cleanliness and good order that reign everywhere throughout the establishment, needs not the turnkey's viva voce explanations to inform the visitor that he is where strict discipline is rigorously enforced, and that the occasional silent fellow-beings who pass and re-pass during his inspection are prisoners of the Crown detained for having in some way or other violated the laws of the land, and are now working out the imprisonment awarded them by their country, in doing little acts of servitude at the bidding of the warders, who are ever on the alert should these temporarily employed prisoners overstep the bounds of their partial freedom, or in any way infringe the strict disciplinary laws of the establishment. But the visitor need not in fact go further than the well barred, and bolted gates to learn this, for as the heavy bolts are withdrawn and the massive iron-bound swings open, a chill seems to creep over you, and the feeling is uppermost in your mind that the residents within are a distinct and separate community shut in, from the outer-world their interests and actions not being akin to those of the busy throng outside, their noticeable (to a visitor) cringing respectful demeanour speaks for itself, of bondage, slavery and crime, having nothing in common with* the outside world, they have an "eye language" peculiarly their own, the shaved cheeks and close cropped heads, speaking without words of the commission, detection, trial, conviction and punishment of crime, reiterating with trumpet voice the now exemplified truth that "the way of transgressors is hard," and almost forcing from your lips the inscription over Dante's Inferno — "Abandon hope, all ye who enter here." On Sunday afternoon by special invitation of the governor (Mr C. G. Thompson), we wended our way along William Street into Ford Street, and soon found (like many more unfortunates) ourselves standing by, while our friend knocked at the gaol gates for admittance. Mr Thompson was quickly at our service, and escorted us through every part of the building.

As the visitor enters from the outer yard before arriving at the lower corridor a long narrow passage about four feet wide leads to the gate of the centre part of the establishment. [...] The peculiarly clean appearance of everything visible to the eye and the painful sense of quietness all around, causing your voice to echo through the corridors and impressers upon your mind the fact that silence is one of the rules of the establishment. There are two long corridors top and bottom, with cells on each side, in the centre of the upper one the "fatal drop" is placed [...] It was here that Smith and Brady were so recently hanged by the neck till dead. But leaving the [...] the "Hangman's trap," we look into a large cell opened by the warder at the bidding of the Governor, and there we see three Chinamen, who, on our entering, stand up in a line and give us the prison salute. These fellows look happy and cheerful, and one of them particularly seemed quite in a [...] mood. No doubt "John" thinks the Victorian treatment of offenders against the law is very different to what is meted out to criminals in the land of flowers and poetry. The appearance of one of the said trio so much resembles a fellow whom we saw receiving the 'cat' at the hands of Bamford in another gaol in the colony, that we are almost inclined to say, "He is the man". But Chinamen as a rule are so "much alike," that it is sometimes impossible to tell 'tother from which, and, in fact, you never can tell," Leaving the three merry Ching Chongs, we peep in to another cell on the opposite side, and see a "prisoner" attentively reading a book. [...] Following our leader, we left this part of the prison and inspected the different yards. The labour yard, where the stone-breakers do their day's work, and the shoemakers, tinkers, carpenters and black-smiths eke out their working hours. We were informed that prisoners as a rule, rather like working at their trades, and always seem more contented and happy when employed at the avocations to which they were accustomed to when free.

The next yard we visited, we found six or seven men in their usual outside-the-gaol-attire, sitting around a large table covered overhead, reading, these we need hardly say were prisoners awaiting trial, the rather shy looking faces, slouched heads with billy-cock hats overhanging the eyebrows, give the visitor an idea that they are as yet not altogether "convicts" and they seemed to think so and felt ashamed of their position. But the most curi-ous place was the "radiating yard," aptly described by a gentleman who was present as the "spoked-wheel yard". Here the warder is placed in a sentry-box in the centre with a look-out to each little yard radiating therefrom, exactly like the spokes of a wheel, so that the Warder on guard can have all the prisoners who are taking their solitary airing under his "ken" at the same time. In walking round this novel exercise ground, we noticed that several of the murderers, executed during the last few years, were buried in this septangular compartment and as the bed rock is no more than three feet from the surface.

We would venture to risk the assertion that the fresh air and exercise to be had by walking up and down these surface cemeteries would be neither pure nor refreshing. On the brick partitions dividing the compartments, we found the initials of four buried murderers, and the number of feet from the wall, all the record left there that underneath lie the bones of the dead. There can be no doubt but these dead-men's yards are a suitable place to exercise criminals in, and to remind them as they walk up and down their allotted space, that there is but a "step between them and the grave." We also had a look at the spot where Smith and Brady were buried. J. S. and T. B., 5 feet, is their only tombstone. Mr Thompson informed us that both these murderers were buried in coffins filled with quick-lime, and that the probabilities are that very little of them now remains, although so recently buried. A turn or two round from these doleful sights brought us to the whipping post, or "triangle, and the modus operandi of using the fasteners was practically illustrated by Mr Thompson. We pity the poor wretch who has to bare his back to the cat-o'-nine-tails used by Bamford. Thus unable to move a limb. We also visited the kitchen, and tasted the "hominy" being prepared for the afternoon meal. It was not at all bad; a large dish of this and a spoonful of dark ration sugar were served to each prisoner. The bread we also examined, and we guess it would take long time to starve on such good wholesome provisions.

After returning to the main building, we were shown the place for "prison worship, and, informed that the Rev. T. Laver officiates regularly, and, that occasional visits are made by the Rev. Father Moran, of the Roman Catholic Church, and the Rev. W. L. C. Howard, of the Church of England, the prisoners as a rule, listen to the spiritual instruction given with great attention, and dissenters of every name attend the Church of England service, and likewise the service by the dissenting minister. We now for the present take our leave of the Beechworth Gaol, feeling as impartial critics, that good management, order, and strict discipline, are the main features of this well conducted establishment, and without fear of contradiction, we assert that a more cleanly kept and better ordered gaol there is not in Victoria, this state of affairs is no doubt owing to the watchful vigilance and excellent management of the Governor, Mr C. G. Thompson.'

Ovens and Murray Advertiser, 11 July 1873. P.2

Notes

Prologue:

- Joe Byrne and Aaron Sherritt taking an unbranded calf into Beechworth. (*Ovens and Murray Advertiser*, 3 *February*, 1876)
- James Warner being the Sherritt family butcher. (*Ovens and Murray Advertiser*, 3 February, 1876.)
- James Warner running a butcher's shop in Camp Street, Beechworth. (*Ovens and Murray Advertiser*, 19 February, 1876)
- Gray and Co. saleyards being in Ford Street, Beechworth. (*Ovens and Murray Advertiser*, 25 June, 1873.)
- Joseph Harvey working as James Warner's slaughterman. (*Ovens and Murray Advertiser*, 3 February, 1876.)
- Aaron Sherritt buying the hide and head of the calf. (*Ovens and Murray Advertiser*, 3 February, 1876.)
- Joe Byrne being known only as 'Burns' by James Warner. (*Ovens and Murray Advertiser*, 3 February, 1876.)

Chapter 1:

- Joe Byrne having a scar on his left shin. (*Victoria Police Gazette* and Ian Jones, *The Fatal Friendship*, 2003, p.41.)

- Edward Kennedy's yard being abandoned and its location behind the Byrne selection. (*Ovens and Murray Advertiser*, 1 June, 1876.)
- Richard Madden being herdsman for El Dorado. (Ovens and Murray Advertiser, 21 November, 1876.)
- Ellen Salisbury being a sweetheart of Joe Byrne's. (*Royal Commission*, Q.13210, p.477.)
- James Salisbury visiting Collier's Beershop. (*Ovens and Murray Advertiser*, 20 February, 1869.)
- Ellen Salisbury marrying Martin Byron. (*Ovens and Murray Advertiser*, 20 July, 1876.)
- Martin Byron being an alcoholic. (*Ovens and Murray Advertiser*, 3 June, 1893.)
- Martin Byron having enemies. (*Ovens and Murray Advertiser*, 15 April, 1876), (*Ovens and Murray Advertiser*, 12 October, 1876) and (*Ovens and Murray Advertiser*, 22 June, 1907.)

Chapter 2:

- Margaret Byrne owning geese. (*Royal Commission*, Q.3608, p.179.)
- Joe Byrne's absence from home. (*Ovens and Murray Advertiser*, 1 June, 1876.)
- Aaron Sherritt's hut at Sheepstation Creek becoming Joe Byrne's refuge. (*The Herald* (Melbourne), 26 July, 1879.)
- Ellen Byrne hardly knowing Joe. (Ian Jones, *The Fatal Friendship*, 2003, p.35.)
- Joe Byrne helping Aaron Sherritt fence his selection. (*Ovens and Murray Advertiser*, 1 June, 1876.)
- Joe Byrne's father, Patrick, dying of heart disease in November 1870. (*Ovens and Murray Advertiser*, 8 November, 1870) and Patrick Byrne's death certificate.
- James Warner going to court for disposing of the unbranded calf's hide. (*Ovens and Murray Advertiser*, 3 February, 1876.)
- Joe Byrne picking up John Phelan's lost saddle. (*Ovens and Murray Advertiser*, 11 December, 1875.)
- The El Dorado School cow's colouration and description of horns. (*Ovens and Murray Advertiser*, 1 June, 1876.)
- James Feely, Kate Byrne's employer, being the owner of the cow. (*Ovens and Murray Advertiser*, 1 June, 1876.)
- Aaron Sherritt using Ah Loy as an alias in order to obtain a butcher's licence. (*Ovens and Murray Advertiser*, 2 November, 1872.)

- Joe going to Mrs. Batchelor for the knife and steel and his reason for needing them. (*Ovens and Murray Advertiser*, 1 June, 1876.)
- Description of the Batchelor house. (*Ovens and Murray Advertiser*, 31 October, 1885.)
- Ellen Salisbury working for the Batchelors as Domestic Servant. (*The Herald* (Melbourne), 26 July, 1879.)
- Only one horse being at Edward Kennedy's yard. (*Ovens and Murray Advertiser*, 1 June, 1876.)
- The cow being slaughtered in Edward Kennedy's yard. (*Ovens and Murray Advertiser*, 1 June, 1876.)
- Dennis Byrne herding goats. (*Ovens and Murray Advertiser*, 1 June, 1876.)
- Andrew Doig witnessing Aaron cut out the heifer's brand and the beast's tongue. (*Ovens and Murray Advertiser*, 1 June, 1876.)
- Joe cutting off the heifer's horns and ears and later placing the head in a zinc trough. (*Ovens and Murray Advertiser*, 1 June 1876.)
- Kate Byrne working as a General Servant for James and Margaret Feely at the Black Springs Hotel. (Ian Jones, *The Fatal Friendship*, 2003, p.35.)
- Paddy Byrne chopping and selling firewood. (Ian Jones, *The Fatal Friendship*, 2003, p.35.)
- Aaron Sherritt sleeping out in the elements without blanket or coat. (Aidan Phelan, *Aaron Sherritt Persona non Grata*, 2022, p.93.)

Chapter 3:

- Joe Byrne being an opium smoker. (*Police telegram*. VPRS 4965/P0000, 354.)
- Joe Byrne and Aaron Sherritt taking a quarter of beef and half the hide to the Sherritt selection. (*Ovens and Murray Advertiser*, 1 June, 1876.)
- John Sherritt cutting strips from the hide. (*Ovens and Murray Advertiser*, 1 June, 1876.)
- Aaron Sherritt tying some of the strips of hide around his hut at Sheepstation Creek. (Ovens and Murray Advertiser, 1 June, 1876.)
- Aaron Sherritt claiming to always beat Joe Byrne in fights. (Aidan Phelan, *Aaron Sherritt Persona non Grata*, 2022, p.93.)
- Constable Mullane and Constable Ward finding Joe Byrne and Aaron Sherritt at the hut at Sheepstation Creek and interrogating them. (*Ovens and Murray Advertiser*, 1 June, 1876.)

- Joe Byrne and Aaron Sherritt being taken back to the Sherritt farm at Sheep-station and further interrogated. (*Ovens and Murray Advertiser*, 1 June, 1876.)
- Joe Byrne and Aaron Sherritt being placed under arrest and taken into Beech-worth with the carcass, head, and legs of the cow. (*Ovens and Murray Advertiser*, 1 June, 1876.)
- Joe Byrne and Aaron Sherritt appearing before Magistrate Pitcairn in Beech-worth. (*Ovens and Murray Advertiser*, 1 June, 1876.)
- Joe Byrne and Aaron Sherritt being locked up in Beechworth Gaol on account of their inability to afford bail. (*Ovens and Murray Advertiser*, 25 May, 1876.)

Chapter 4:

- Margaret Byrne being unable to say if Joe Byrne is kind to her during the trial. (*Ovens and Murray Advertiser*, 1 June, 1876.)
- Joe Byrne and Aaron Sherritt sentenced to 6 months in Beechworth Gaol with hard labour. (*Ovens and Murray Advertiser*, 1 June, 1876.)
- Joe Byrne's measurements. (Ian Jones, The Fatal Friendship, 2003, p.41.)

Chapter 5:

- Joe Byrne's letter to Jack Sherritt. (VPRS 4969/P0000, 18.)

Joe Byrne c.~1877, photographed by Bray of Beechworth.
Private Collection

Aaron Sherritt, c.~1876, photographed by Bray of Beechworth.
Burke Museum, Beechworth

Margaret Byrne c.1870s, photographed by Bray of Beechworth.
Private Collection

Archibald and Jane Batchelor, c.1870s
Private Collection

"Eldorado (Vic)" by S. Foxcroft Photography, c.1900. In background from right :- El Dorado
State School (est.1869), Wesleyan Church (c.1868), St. Augustine's Church (c.1868)
Courtesy: El Dorado Museum Association

Closer view of the school.

1872—El Dorado School No. 246.

El Dorado State School, c.1872.
Courtesy: El Dorado Museum Association

The school as it appears now. It currently houses the El Dorado Museum.
Courtesy: Aidan Phelan

Beechworth, c.1870s
Courtesy: State Library Victoria; 9917155733607636

El Dorado, c.1900
Courtesy: El Dorado Museum Association

Remains of the Beechworth lock-up.
Author's Collection

The dock, Beechworth courthouse
Author's Collection

99

No. 13890.   Name Byrne Joseph

Height ... 5f 9in   Sentence Imprisonment
Weight ...   H—
Complexion ... Fair
Hair ... Brown
Eyes ... Blue
Nose ...   Date of
Mouth ...   Conviction 30. 5. 76
Chin ...
Eyebrows ...   Offence Unlawful
Visage ...   possession of the
Forehead ...   carcass of a cow.
Date of Birth ... 1857
Native Place ... Victoria   Where and   Beechworth
Trade ... Labour   taken when   Petty Sess
Religion ... R. Catholic   th
Read or Write ... Both   of Bench

    Particular Marks.

    Previous History.

At what District.   When   Offence, Sentence, &c.
                     received
Beechworth Gaol 30. 5. 76.

            Prison record of Joe Byrne
        Courtesy: Public Records Office, Victoria

No. *13891.*   Name *Sherritt Aaron.*

Height _ ft 10in	Sentence _ Six Months					
Weight _	Hd.					
Complexion _ Fresh						
Hair _ Brown						
Eyes _ Hazel						
Nose _	Date of Conviction _ 30 . 5 . 76.					
Mouth _						
Chin _						
Eyebrows _	Crimes _ Unlawful					
Vision _	possession of the					
Forehead _	carcase of a cow.					
Date of Birth _ 1856						
Native place _ Victoria	Where and before whom tried _ Beechworth					
Trade _ Labour	Petty Sess					
Religion _ Ch of Engl	Cd					
Read or Write _ Both	of Bench.					

Peculiar Marks

Previous History

At what Station.	When received.	Offences, Sentences, &c.	Visiting Justice.		Superintendent.	
			M.	D.	M.	D.
Beechworth Gaol	30.5.76					

Exterior of the Beechworth Gaol as it appears now.
Author's Collection

Interior of Beechworth Gaol
Author's Collection

The Author

Georgina Stones was born and raised in Tasmania, but has recently made the move across Bass Strait to reside in Victoria. She has a love of history, with the lives of Australian outlaws Joe Byrne and Michael Howe her main interests in that field.

She attended school in Ulverstone and has since studied journalism through Deakin University. Her natural inquisitiveness and perseverance have paid off in her work on *An Outlaw's Journal*, uncovering many previously forgotten or overlooked aspects of the life of Joe Byrne, particularly in regards to his early life and connections to the Chinese community.

She also researches and writes for her website *Michael Howe: Governor of the Woods* for which she has been interviewed on ABC Radio and featured in Traces magazine.

The Illustrator

Aidan Phelan is the writer and historian for A Guide to Australian Bushranging, which has been bringing Australia's outlaw heritage to a worldwide audience since 2017. In 2021 he was featured in a series of interviews on ABC Radio Hobart and Northern Tasmania discussing the history of bushrangers in Tasmania, and was interviewed for The Hobart Magazine about bushranger "Rocky" Whelan.

He has also worked as an illustrator, contributing work for Judy Lawson's The Clarke Bushrangers: A Clash of Cultures in 2020, and regularly provides illustrations for An Outlaw's Journal by Georgina Stones.

In 2020 he self-published his first novel, Glenrowan, which dramatised the final months of the Kelly Outbreak. He is also developing Glenrowan as a television miniseries with filmmaker Matthew Holmes (The Legend of Ben Hall).

The Outlaw

Joseph Byrne was born to Irish parents in Victoria, Australia, around 1856/57. His father died when Joe was just a boy and he soon looked for work around the Woolshed Valley, where he lived. He spent much of his time with the Chinese in Sebastopol and Beechworth, and with his best friend Aaron Sherritt.

In his early twenties, Joe joined Aaron and Ned Kelly in a horse stealing operation, before being implicated in the police murders at Stringybark Creek in 1878, alongside Ned Kelly, Dan Kelly and Steve Hart. Joe was outlawed, eventually gaining a reward for his capture of £2000. He was an accomplice in two bank robberies and after being coerced into murdering Aaron, was killed during a siege at Glenrowan on 26 June 1880. He is buried in Benalla cemetery.

www.ingramcontent.com/pod-product-compliance
Lightning Source LLC
Chambersburg PA
CBHW031930090426
42811CB00002B/141